Daily
Learning
Drills

Grade 1

BRIGHTER CHILD ®

Columbus, Ohio

Table of Contents

Name _____

The Alphabet

____✏️ a line to connect the dots. Follow the letters of the alphabet.

Start here.

A
Z
B
X
Y
D
C
E
V
U
G
F
W
T
H
S
I
R
J
Q
K
L
P
N
O
M

Name _____

Under-Cover Work

Color the pictures. Then cut them out and glue onto Ira's sleeping bag in ABC order.

dinner

suitcase

bear

Reggie

pillow

flashlight

Name _____

The Quail Trail

Read the words. Cut and paste them on the quails in alphabetical order.

Cut -

America   kind   quail   wonderful

gathered   Thanksgiving   courage   joy   ready

Name _____

Squeeze a Summer Sipper

Read the words on the juicer. Write them in alphabetical order.

Word Bank

school	apples	leaves
working	playing	blossoms
town	clothes	mowing

1 _____

2 _____

3 _____

4 _____

5 _____

6 _____

7 _____

8 _____

9 _____

Name _____

Morris Learns the Alphabet

To help Morris find his way to the candy store write the words from the Word Bank in ABC order.

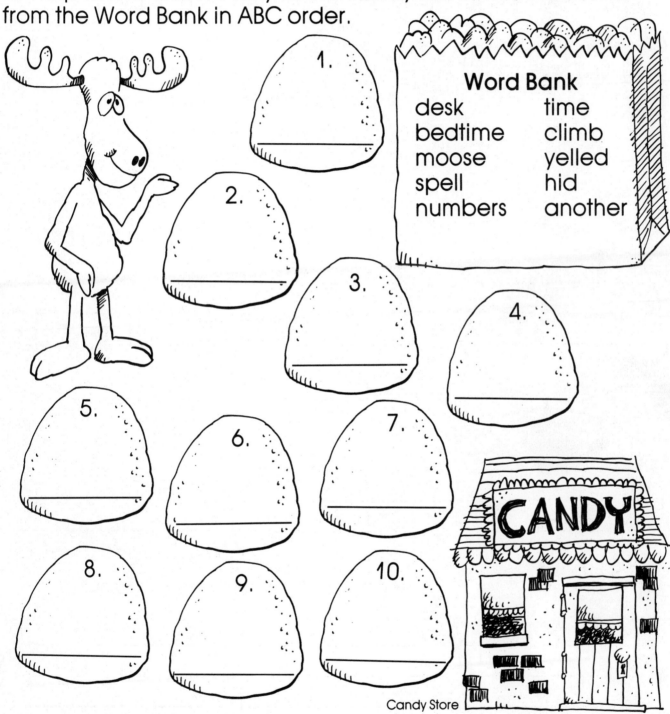

Word Bank

desk	time
bedtime	climb
moose	yelled
spell	hid
numbers	another

1.

2.

3.

4.

5.

6.

7.

8.

9.

10.

Candy Store

CANDY

Name _____

Ghosts and Spaceships

Write the words in ABC order on the correct picture.

Color space word boxes red and blue.
Color Halloween word boxes orange and black.

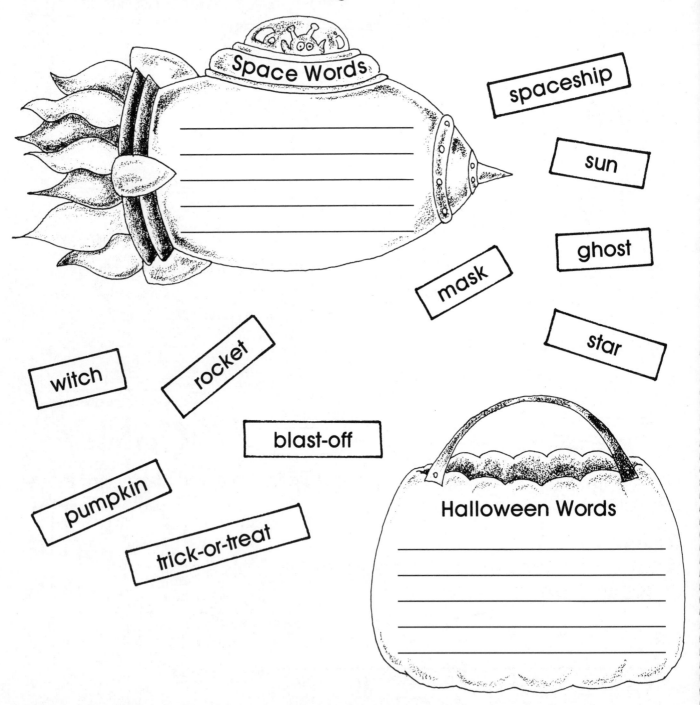

Name _____

Alpha-bear-tical Antics

Follow the directions to answer the riddle below. In each paw, print the letter that comes...

1. Between H and J

6. Before S

7. After K

2. After G

3. Before N

8. Before B

4. After A

9. Between D and F

5. Between S and U

Now answer the riddle by writing the letter from each paw print in the space above the same number.

Riddle

What famous lady bear was the first to fly across the Atlantic Ocean?

___ ___ ___ ___ ___ ___
 8   3   9   7   1   8

___ ___ ___ ___ ___ ___ ___ ___
 4   9   8   6   2   8   6   5

Name _____

Letter Lift

Cut out the letter squares. Paste each square on the correct balloon.

o s m a q h d o r j x p

f g t i l b e n v u c k

Name _____

"Feast" Your Eyes on This!

Look at the picture. Find and circle the letters that are hidden in the picture that spell **Happy Thanksgiving**. Color the picture.

Name _____

Sea Search

Help the boat sail to the island! Color the fish:

capital letters—orange   **lower-case letters**—blue

Take One or Two

Name _____

Look at each picture on the cookies and read the word below it. Cut and paste each cookie on the correct jar to show how many syllables are in the word.

1 Syllable

2 Syllables

Cut _____

mop

stinkweed

mailbox

heart

paintbrush

sparkles

card

cut

bathtub

hug

Daily Learning Drills Grade 1

Name _____

Two for the Dragon

Cut out the muffins. Glue the six muffins with two-syllable words on the dragon's tummy. Glue the rest in the center of another sheet of drawing paper. Then create and color your own dragon around these muffins.

king

poor

drawbridge

dragon

firewood

muncher

flour

bake

kingdom

villagers

bowl

muffin

Bonus

Fill these muffins with your own two-syllable words.

Name _____

Half a Zoo

McGrew needs your help to capture the other half of these new zoo animals. Draw a matching half for each picture on this page. Color.

Elephant-Cat

Obsk

Tick-Tack-Toe

Iota

Name _____

Warm and Cozy

Look at the picture very carefully. All of the animals are snuggled in different places. Circle the eight animals hidden in the picture. Then color the picture.

rabbit   badger   duck   mouse

mole   hedgehog   fox   squirrel

Name _____

Hidden Pebble Search

Sylvester hid 20 magic pebbles in this picture. Find the pebbles. Color them red and circle them with black. Then color the rest of the picture.

Name _____

Snowy Day

Circle the mistakes in this crazy, snowy-day picture. Then color all parts of the picture.

Name _____

Select a Synonym

Read the words. ✏ the word that means almost the same as the first word.

1. big		cold	loud	large
2. yell		shout	eat	jump
3. small		good	thin	little
4. smile		tall	grin	soft
5. boat		talk	ship	hop
6. look		see	fall	laugh

Name _____

Similar Meanings

Read the words in the word box. two words under each picture.

rock	start	road	begin	street	stone
shut	sad	talk	unhappy	speak	closed

_____

_____

_____

_____

_____

_____

Name _____

A Change in the Weather

Change Alexander's cloudy day into a sunny day! Cut and paste an opposite in the ☼ for each ☁ word.

Word Bank

happy   play   night   cold   outside

Name _____

Attach an Antonym

Read the word on each person. Find the word above the hair that means the opposite and paste it on that head.

cold   work   same   boring

wet   in   happy   you

Cut -

dry   out   different   sad

exciting   me   hot   play

In or Out?

Name _____

Read the words. Find a word in the Word Bank that means the opposite of each word given. Then write it on the line.

1. up   _____
2. in   _____
3. sad   _____
4. stop   _____
5. big   _____
6. on   _____
7. left   _____
8. here   _____
9. yes   _____
10. mother   _____

Word Bank

out	little	there
go	happy	no
down	large	off
mom	right	father

Name _____

Same or Opposite?

Color the spaces yellow that have word pairs with opposite meanings. Color the spaces blue that have word pairs with the same meanings.

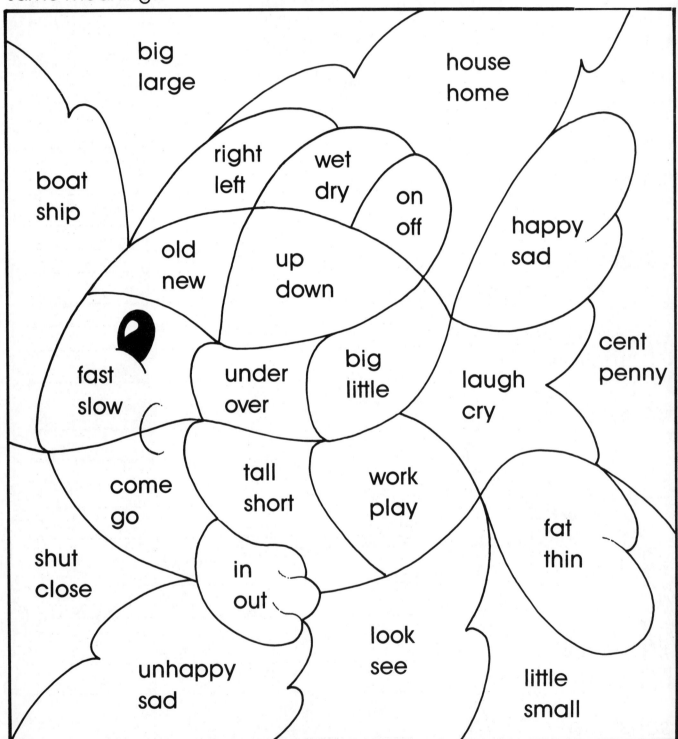

big
large

house
home

boat
ship

right
left

wet
dry

on
off

old
new

up
down

happy
sad

fast
slow

under
over

big
little

laugh
cry

cent
penny

come
go

tall
short

work
play

fat
thin

shut
close

in
out

look
see

unhappy
sad

little
small

Name _____

Two Words in One

 the two words that make up each compound word below.

snowball

_____ _____

raincoat

_____ _____

airplane

_____ _____

watermelon

_____ _____

haircut

_____ _____

football

_____ _____

fingernail

_____ _____

sunshine

_____ _____

Daily Learning Drills Grade 1

Name _____

It's Raining Meatballs!

Draw a line from each word in List A to a word in List B to make a compound word. On another piece of paper, write the compound words and draw pictures of them.

List A

List B

Name _____

"Compound"-ing the Cave's Echo

Read the words in the Word Bank. Find the two words that go together to make a compound word and write it on a bat.

bath	bed	bee
birth	by	comb
cow	day	every
fire	flies	for
got	grass	hide
hive	honey	lands
lights	near	
one	room	
spread	street	

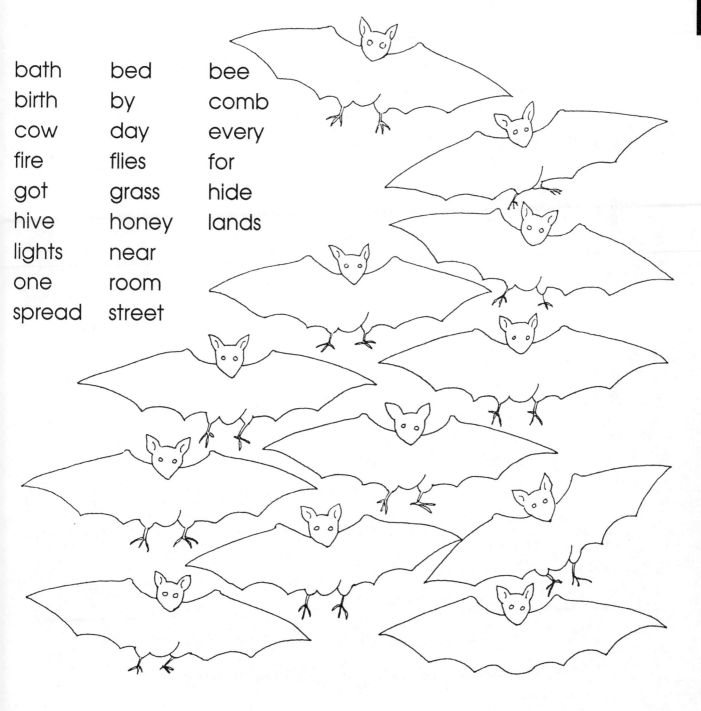

Daily Learning Drills Grade 1

Name _____

Let's Make a Snowman

a line from each pair of words to the right contraction.

he is •   • it's

it is •   • she's

she is •   • he's

they are •   • you're

you are •   • they're

we are •   • I'm

I am •   • we're

Loppy Ears

Name _____

A contraction is a short way to write two words. Choose a contraction from the big carrot and print it on the lines.

1. Leo _____ get his ears to stand up tall.

2. _____ not fun to be teased by the others.

3. "_____ not normal," thought Leo.

4. Doing ear exercises _____ help Leo.

5. _____ go see the possum, he'll know what to do.

6. _____ my good friend.

7. The other bunnies _____ get their ears to flop down.

8. _____ all normal because we are loved.

I'm   We're   couldn't   can't   He's   didn't

I'll   It's

Name _____

"Crumb"-y Contractions

Read the two words on the bread crumbs. Find the contraction in the Word Bank and write it on the bird.

we   are

that   is

I   would

I   will

she   is

they   are

she   would

let   us

we   would

we'd	she's
let's	I'll
I'd	we're

they're

that's

she'd

Name _____

Barnyard Nouns

| A noun is a naming word. |
| A noun names a person, place or thing. |

Find **two** nouns in each sentence below.

 them.

1. The pig has a curly tail.	
2. The hen is sitting on her nest.	
3. A horse is in the barn.	
4. The goat has horns.	
5. The cow has a calf.	
6. The farmer is painting the fence.	

Daily Learning Drills Grade I

Name _____

Nouns on the Farm

Read the naming words below. ~~✎ the correct naming word for each picture of a person, place or thing.

barn   farmer   pig
boy   tree   horse
girl   ducks   sun

Name _____

LANGUAGE ARTS

Action Match

Find the action word in each sentence. it.
___ a line to match each sentence with the correct picture.

1. The dog barks.

2. The bird flies.

3. A fish swims.

4. One monkey swings.

5. A turtle crawls.

6. A boy talks.

Daily Learning Drills Grade 1

Name _____

Circus Action

Find the verb in each sentence below and ✏ it.

1. The bear climbs a ladder.

2. Two tiny dogs dance.

3. A boy eats cotton candy.

4. A woman swings on a trapeze.

5. The clown falls down.

6. A tiger jumps through a ring.

Name _____

Falling Verbs

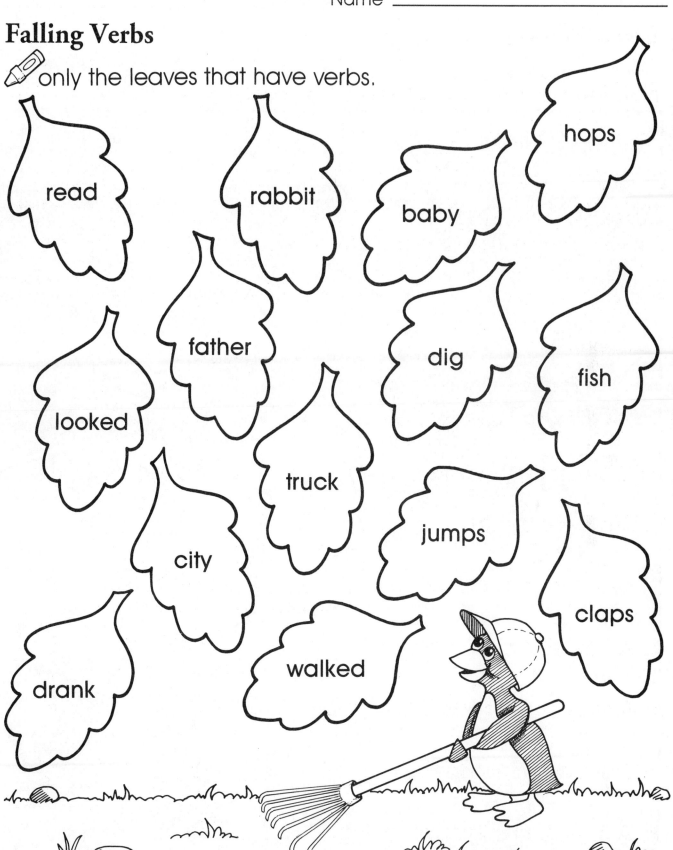 only the leaves that have verbs.

read

rabbit

baby

hops

father

looked

dig

fish

truck

city

jumps

claps

drank

walked

Daily Learning Drills Grade I

Name _____

Am I a Noun or a Verb?

Color the spaces with **naming** words green. Color the spaces with **action** words pink.

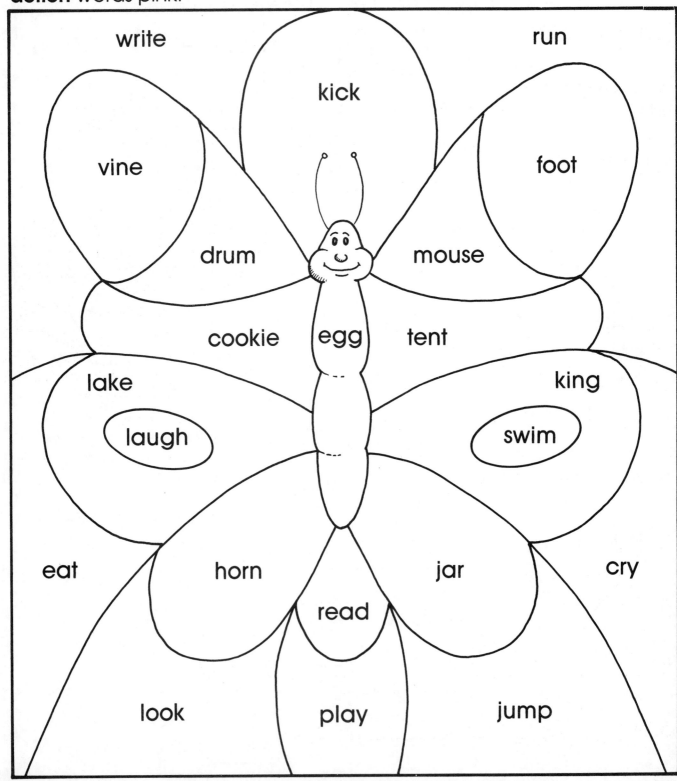

Name _____

Animal Adjectives

 a describing word in each sentence below.
Use the word bank to help you.

Word Bank

big   bushy   three
round   green   six

1. A has a _____ tail.

2. A has _____ legs.

3. The will become a _____ frog.

4. A has _____ teeth.

5. _____ hang by their tails.

6. An has _____ eyes.

Name _____

Fishing for Adjectives

only the fish with describing words.

Name _____

Corn Crackles

Here are some describing words:

sour	furry	sweet	tasty	crisp
tall	crunchy	cloudy	sad	soft

Which four words do you think might best describe the cereal? ✏️ them on the lines on the cereal box.

16 oz.

CORN CRACKLES

Surprise inside!

Puzzle on back!

Name _____

The Turtles Tell

> Some sentences tell something.
> Telling sentences begin with a capital letter.
> Telling sentences end with a period.

only the sentences that tell.

1. Two turtles sat on a log.

2. One turtle fell off.

3. Did you see him?

4. He swam away.

5. The water is cold.

6. Can you swim?

Name _____

All About Dinosaurs

 the telling sentences below. Begin each
sentence with a capital letter and end with a period.

1. dinosaurs lived long ago

_____

- -

_____

2. many were very big

_____

- -

_____

3. some dinosaurs ate plants

_____

- -

_____

4. all the dinosaurs died out

_____

- -

_____

5. no one is sure why

_____

- -

_____

Name _____

State It!

> Some sentences tell something. They are called statements. A statement begins with a capital letter and ends with a period.

✏ these statements correctly.

1. jenny planted a seed

_____

- - - - - - - - - - - - - - - - - - -

_____

2. she gave it water

_____

- - - - - - - - - - - - - - - - - - -

_____

3. it sat in the sunshine

_____

- - - - - - - - - - - - - - - - - - -

_____

4. the plant began to grow

_____

- - - - - - - - - - - - - - - - - - -

_____

5. leaves grew large

_____

- - - - - - - - - - - - - - - - - - -

_____

6. a flower opened

_____

- - - - - - - - - - - - - - - - - - -

_____

Fishy Questions

Name _____

 the first word of each question below.
Remember to begin with a capital letter. End each
question with a question mark.

1. _____ that your boat___
   (is)

2. _____ you catch that fish___
   (did)

3. _____ much does it weigh___
   (how)

4. _____ you eat it___
   (will)

5. _____ you fish with worms___
   (did)

6. _____ the water cold___
   (is)

Daily Learning Drills Grade 1

Name _____

Did You Ask Me Something?

Some sentences ask something. They are called questions. A question begins with a capital letter and ends with a question mark.

only the questions.

1. Is that your house?

2. There are two pictures on the wall.

3. Where do you sleep?

4. Do you watch TV in that room?

5. Which coat is yours? _____

6. The kitten is asleep.

Name _____

Period or Question Mark?

SNAKES
$29.95

GOLDFISH
$1.98

TURTLE $3.75

Put a period or a question mark at the end of each sentence.

1. Can the fish jump out of the tank ☐

2. Two snakes are in that cage ☐

3. How much does that turtle cost ☐

4. Yes, I already have a dog ☐

5. His name is King ☐

6. Do you have a dog ☐

LANGUAGE ARTS

Name _____

Pick a Pouch

Cut and paste each word on the correct kangaroo pouch. Then color one kangaroo green and the other your favorite color.

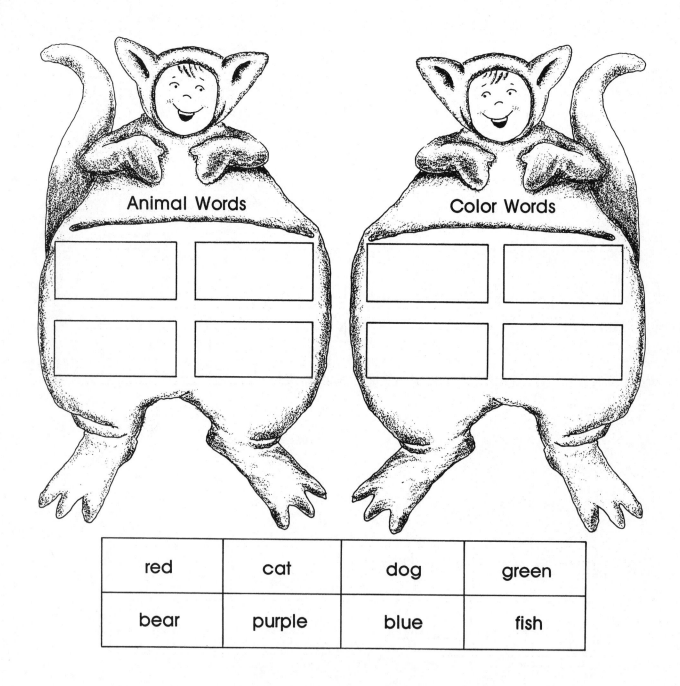

Animal Words

Color Words

red	cat	dog	green
bear	purple	blue	fish

Name _____

Pick a Pouch

Cut and paste each word on the correct kangaroo pouch. Then color one kangaroo green and the other your favorite color.

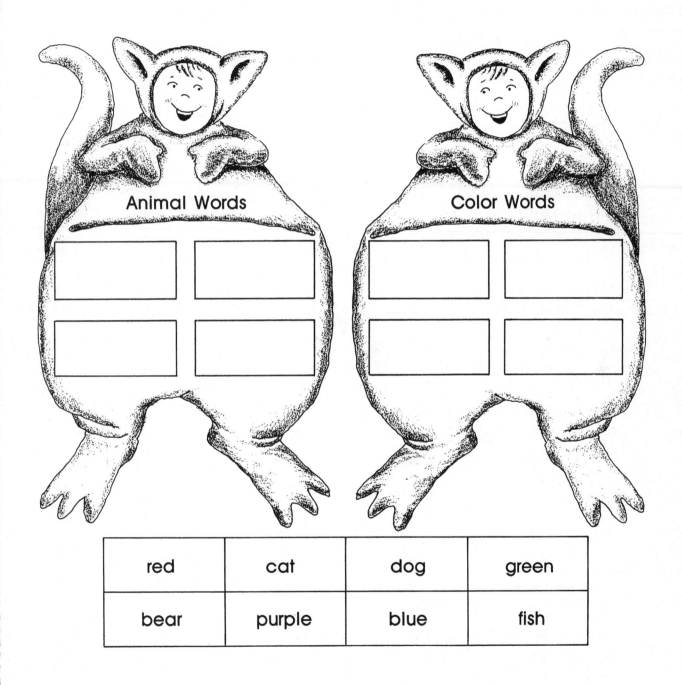

Animal Words

Color Words

red	cat	dog	green
bear	purple	blue	fish

"Cap" the Words

Name _____

Read the headings on the caps. Write the words from the Word Bank on the correct cap.

How Clothes Can Feel

_____
_____
_____
_____
_____
_____

Words That Tell Where

_____
_____
_____
_____
_____

Which word is left over? _____

Word Bank

under	over	hot
warm	itchy	in
jacket	stiff	on

Name _____

Cake Faces

Cut and paste the words where they belong.

Names

Types of Costumes

Things That Are Fun

How Costumes Look

Cut -

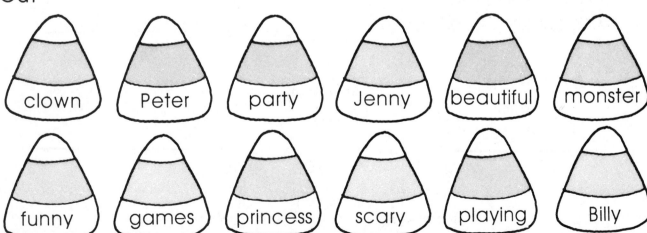

clown   Peter   party   Jenny   beautiful   monster

funny   games   princess   scary   playing   Billy

Name _____

Missing Pieces

Write the puzzle words on the correct lines. Color the pieces as shown.

People purple

_____   _____
_____   _____

Things in a Hospital   red

_____   _____
_____   _____

Food   yellow

_____   _____
_____   _____

Places   green

_____   _____
_____   _____

Toys   blue

_____   _____
_____   _____

Name _____

Pumpkin Patch Pick

Read. Cut and paste each picture where it belongs.

The pumpkin is in the wagon.

The ladybug is on the sprout.

The butterfly is on the flower.

The seeds are in Jamie's hand.

Cut —

Daily Learning Drills Grade 1

Name _____

Down on the Farm

A farm is a home for some animals. Horses, cows and pigs live on a farm. Sheep and chickens are farm animals, too. Many farm animals live in a big barn.

Which animals live on a farm?

_____ ride   farm _____

- - - - - - - - - -

A _____ is a home for some animals.

Many farm animals live in a big

barn.

• Draw and color two farm animals.

Name _____

My Pet

It is fun to have a pet. Dogs and cats are good pets. Birds and rabbits can be pets, too. Pets are good friends. They need care and love every day.

friends	fast

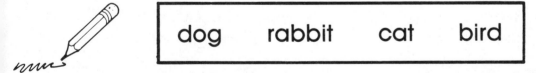

Pets are good _____ .

Pets need care and   long.
love.

dog   rabbit   cat   bird

• Draw and color a picture of your pet.

Name _____

Mixed-up Colors

Did you know that all colors come from red, yellow or blue? They're the primary colors. Red and blue make purple. Blue and yellow make green. Yellow and red make orange. It is fun to mix paint to make new colors.

Circle.

Which three colors do you need to make all colors?

red   green   yellow   blue   pink

Write.

Red, yellow and blue are _____ colors.

orange   primary

Match.

Red and blue make   orange.

Blue and yellow make   purple.

Yellow and red make   green.

Color the picture: **1** - red   **2** - yellow   **3** - blue

4 - orange   **5** - purple   **6** - green

• Draw and color a picture using the **primary** colors.

Name _____

Scrambled Shoes

Minnie needs new shoes. She tries on several pairs and decides on one pair. Oops! While trying on all of the shoes, she has scattered them all over. Now she can't find the other shoe of the pair she wants.

Help Minnie find her shoe. Using a different color for each pair of shoes, color each pair exactly the same. Then draw a circle around Minnie's missing shoe.

Name _____

Barbecue Mishap

Meg and her family are barbecuing hamburgers. A gust of wind blows the flames toward a tree. Oh no! The tree is on fire! A fire truck races to the fire.

Trace the different ways the firefighters can get to Meg's house.

How many different ways did you find? _____

Use a red crayon to trace the quickest way to Meg's house.

Name _____

Musician's Choice

Many different instruments are used to make music. Irene knows how to play several musical instruments.

Irene knows how to play these instruments.

Irene does not know how to play these instruments.

Draw a circle around the instruments Irene probably also knows how to play.

LANGUAGE ARTS

Name _____

Family Portraits

Families may be big or small. No matter how many people are in a family, each person is important to the others.

Cut out the pictures at the bottom of the page. Read the clues. Paste the pictures of the members of this family in the frame where they belong.

- Grandfather is in the middle.
- The girl is on the right end.
- The boy is on the left end.
- Mother is between Grandmother and the boy.
- Father is beside the girl.
- The family dog is between Grandfather and Father.

Name _____

Where Is That Sheep?

Read. Cut and paste each sheep where it belongs. Color the pictures.

The sheep is on the table. 	The sheep is under the loom.
The sheep is in the pokeweed berry bush. 	The sheep is beside the cloth.
The sheep is on Charlie's hat. 	The sheep is in between the pieces of Charlie's cloak.

Cut -

Daily Learning Drills Grade 1

Umbrellas Up!

Name _____

Look at the pictures. Circle the correct word and write it on the line.

Molly puts _____ the

umbrella.

up   on   in

The tie is _____ the

bed.

up   on   in

The cat is _____ the

house.

up   on   in

The bird flies _____

up   on   in

He puts _____

mittens.

up   on   in

The dog is _____ the

rain.

up   on   in

Name _____

Playing Parts

Look at each picture. Find the title of the story that Grace is acting out in the Word Bank. Write it under the correct picture.

_____

- - - - - - - - - - - - - - - - - -

_____

- - - - - - - - - - - - - - - - - -

_____

- - - - - - - - - - - - - - - - - -

_____

- - - - - - - - - - - - - - - - - -

_____

Word Bank

The Case of the Missing Cat	Cowboy Jake & the Roundup
Space Adventures	The Lost Treasure Chest

LANGUAGE ARTS

Name _____

It's Time to . . .

✂ and 🖌 four sentences under the correct pictures.

| Susie's alarm clock rings. | Susie picks up her books. |
| Susie is getting hungry. | Susie hears the school bell ring. |

It's time to go home from school. | It's time to get up.

It's time to go to sleep. | It's time to go to school.

It's time to eat lunch. | It's time to paint the fence.

Name _____

What Will They Do?

Read each sentence and question. _____ a ✓ in the box by the correct answer. _____ a picture to answer the question.

The boy is putting on his skates.

What will he do?

☐ He will go swimming.

☐ He will go skating.

Draw.

The girl fills her glass with milk.

What will she do?

☐ She will drink the milk.

☐ She will drop the milk.

Draw.

The lady wrote a letter to her friend.

What will she do?

☐ She will throw the letter away.

☐ She will mail the letter.

Draw.

The kids gave Sally a birthday gift.

What will she do?

☐ She will open the gift.

☐ She will not open the gift.

Draw.

Name _____

What Does That Mean?

Read. Color the picture that shows what each sentence **really** means.

We are just horsing around.

Pipe down, please.

The window flew open.

She had a puzzled look.

He is down in the dumps.

Name _____

Save Six

Color six animals.

Color six things that will grow.

Draw pictures of six of your favorite things on the back of this paper.

Name _____

Where's the Hair?

Draw different kinds of hair on each head. Color.

Suited for Winter

Name _____

Read and do.

1. Draw a hat on the snowman. Color the hat **purple** and **orange**.

2. Draw a snowsuit on the snowman. Color the snowsuit **blue.**

3. Draw boots on the snowman. Color the boots **yellow**.

4. Draw mittens on the snowman. Color the mittens **green**.

Name _____

Meet the Alien

1. Color the hands ✋ and arms ◯ yellow.
2. Print your name on the biggest ▭ .
3. Draw a red ⌣ on the face.
4. Put green dots on the ◠ .
5. Color the 🖐 purple.
6. Color all of the △ 's orange.
7. Draw red and blue stripes on the legs ◯ .
8. Color the ☐ blue.

Name _____

What's the Idea?

Read the sentence in each speech bubble. Underline the main idea.

May I have more ice cream?

She likes cake best.
She likes ice cream a lot.

Daily Learning Drills Grade 1

Name _____

Yes or No?

Read each sentence. Circle **yes** if the sentence tells about the picture. Circle **no** if it does not.

yes   no

The running shoe is very old.

yes   no

The tree has lost its leaves.

yes   no

The soup smells good.

yes   no

Two butterflies sit on flowers.

yes   no

The dog eats a new bone.

yes   no

The boy sees the plane.

yes   no

The snake is lying on a rock.

yes   no

The spider is spinning its web.

Name _____

Picture Pick

Look at each picture. Read the sentences. the correct letter in each ◯ to tell the main idea.

A-The eggs are ready to hatch.

B-It is a very windy day.

C-The old house is very spooky.

D-The popcorn popper is too full.

E-The girl thinks the music is too loud.

F-It is too warm for a snowman.

 the pictures:

A —yellow
B —red
C —blue
D —green
E —orange
F —purple

Daily Learning Drills Grade 1

Name _____

What About Bear?

Read each sentence. Circle **yes** if the sentence tells about the picture. Circle **no** if it does not.

yes   no

It is a very hot day.

yes   no

The hat is too small.

yes   no

The bear is afraid of the mouse.

yes   no

The bear washed three shirts.

yes   no

The circus is lots of fun.

yes   no

The bear has two mittens.

yes   no

The bear walks to school.

yes   no

The bear likes to cook.

Name _____

What Did Morris Do Now?

Look at the pictures. Find the sentence in the Word Bank that matches each picture. Write it on the lines.

_____

_____

_____

_____

_____

_____

Word Bank

Morris hid his gumdrops.

Morris was too big for the desk.

Morris wanted to go home.

Morris was too little for the desk.

Morris pretended to be a closet.

What a Life!

Name _____

Read each sentence. If it tells something that could really happen, paste it under the real dog. If it tells something that is make-believe, paste it under the make-believe dog.

Cut -

A dog can fly a kite.	A dog can walk on a sidewalk.
A dog can sit beneath a tree.	A dog can be a lead singer.
A dog can splash in the water.	A dog puts jam on toast.
A dog can row a boat.	A dog likes to eat bones.

Name _____

My Friend the Bear

Read each sentence. If it tells something that could really happen, color the real bear. If it tells something that is make-believe, color the toy bear.

Real   **Make-Believe**

1. A bear can live in a forest.

2. A bear can search in a store for a lost button.

3. A girl can sew a button on a pair of overalls.

4. A bear can talk to a little girl.

5. A toy bear can ride up an escalator by himself.

6. A toy bear can sit on a toy department shelf.

7. A little girl can save money in a piggy bank.

8. A toy bear and a little girl can be friends.

9. A toy bear can yank a button off a mattress.

Go for the Snow

Name _____

Read the word on each mitten. Find the word on a snowball that rhymes with it. Cut and paste the snowball on the correct mitten. Color the mittens.

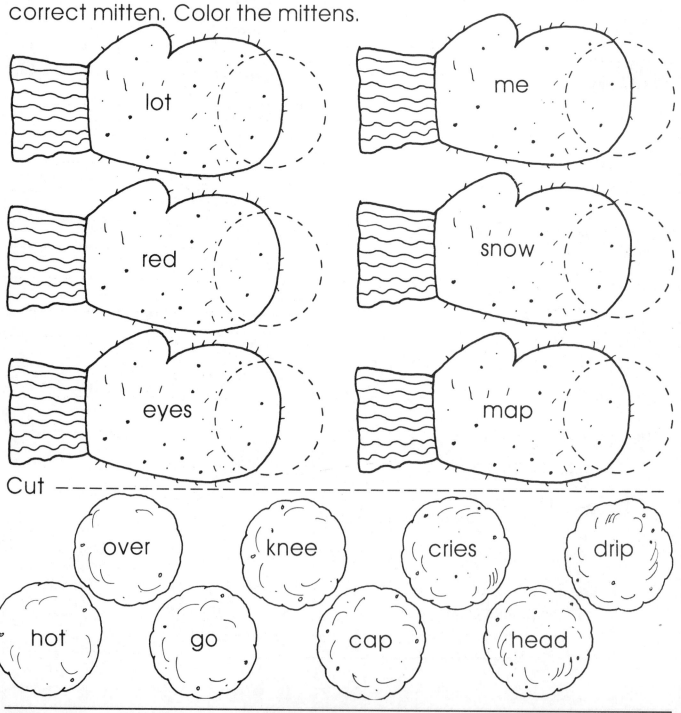

lot

me

red

snow

eyes

map

Cut —

over

knee

cries

drip

hot

go

cap

head

Name _____

Strawberry Patch Match

Read the word on each strawberry. Find the word in the
Word Bank that rhymes. Write it on the line.

sun _____

sky _____

bark _____

kite _____

flowers _____

Sam _____

day _____

goat _____

tea _____

cool _____

Word Bank

away	boat	high	fun
might	park	tree	jam
	showers	school	

Name _____

A Space Case!

Read the word on each spaceship. Find the words in the Word Bank that rhyme and write them on the line.

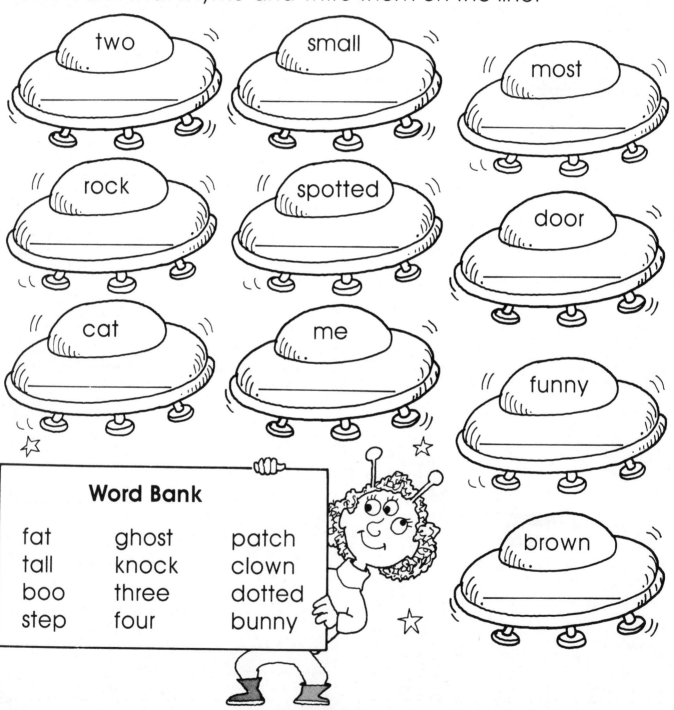

Word Bank

fat	ghost	patch
tall	knock	clown
boo	three	dotted
step	four	bunny

Name _____

Carrot Crop

 the four pictures. ✂ and 🧹 the pictures in **1, 2, 3, 4** order.

Daily Learning Drills Grade 1

Name _____

Fall Pick Up

Color the pictures. Cut and paste each picture in 1, 2, 3, 4 order.

It's Hard to Wait!

Name _____

Write 1, 2, 3, or 4 in the boot next to the picture to show the order it happened in the story. Then draw a line from the boot to the sentence that tells about that picture.

He has a new snowsuit.

He made a snowball.

He put on his new snowsuit, boots, hat and mittens.

He wished and wished for snow.

Name _____

How Many?

Read the words in the Word Bank. If the word means one,
write it under Buster. If the word means more than one, write it
under Sue Ellen.

one

1. _____
2. _____
3. _____
4. _____
5. _____
6. _____

more than one

1. _____
2. _____
3. _____
4. _____
5. _____
6. _____

Word Bank

teeth	child	class	people
straw	men	children	tooth
babies	person	recess	patients

Name _____

Animal Chatter

Unscramble the letters and the name of each animal. the correct animal sound in each ☁.

squeak   baa   gobble   moo   quack   meow   roar

o i l n   e m u o s   c d k u

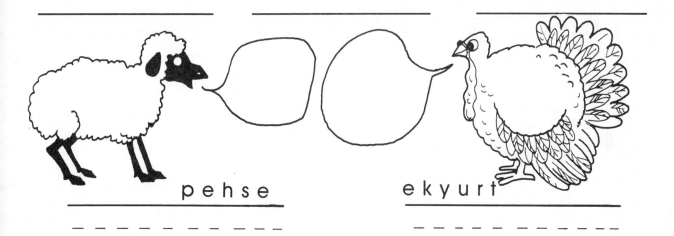

p e h s e   e k y u r t

w c o   t n i t k e

Daily Learning Drills Grade 1

Name _____

Size Search

Circle each size word. Write the correct number by each picture.
Color each picture the correct color.

1. a long, brown snake.

2. a little, red heart.

3. a tall, green tree.

4. a large, blue house.

5. a small, orange gift.

6. a short, yellow pencil.

7. a big, purple tent.

Name _____

Confection Perfection

Cut out the pictures of the candy at the bottom of the page. Paste the pictures to correctly continue the pattern in each row.

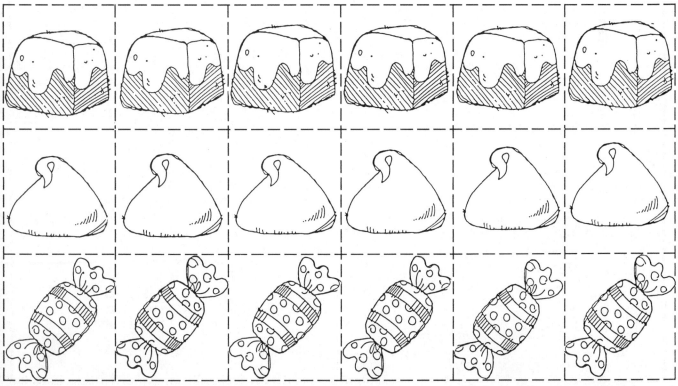

Daily Learning Drills Grade 1

Name _____

Roaring Roller-Coaster Rides

Cut out the roller coaster cars at the bottom of the page. Paste them to correctly continue the pattern on each track.

Name _____

Strawberry Stack-Up

Farmers grow ripe, red strawberries for everyone to eat. Before taking the strawberries to the stores, the farmers put them in small baskets.

Look at the pattern of the baskets in each row. Draw the correct number of strawberries in the baskets to continue each pattern.

Name _____

Stringing It Along

Complete each pattern. Color the red and the pink.

Name _____

Special Hearts for a Special Friend

Look at the picture carefully.

How many hearts were used to draw the cat? _____

Draw and color a picture of an animal using only heart shapes.

Name _____

Animal Action

Find the shapes and color the picture using the code.

○ red   ☐ blue   ▭ yellow

△ green   ◇ orange   ⬭ black

Name _____

Cabin to Capitol

Abraham Lincoln was the 16th president of the United States. He was born in a log cabin. Many people lived in log cabins at that time.

Look at this picture of a log cabin. How many of each of the different shapes can you find in the picture?

How many 's? _____   How many ⬭ 's? _____

How many 's? _____   Draw and color a door.

Daily Learning Drills Grade 1

Name _____

Mask Make-Up

Masks have been made by people for many years. In some countries, the actors in plays wear masks. Masks can be made from wood, metal, paper, cloth, or even foil. They can be painted with a design or a face. Color the mask by using the color code.

◯ **red**   ▢ **orange**   △ **yellow**   ▭ **blue**

Name _____

Animal Shapes

Color:

squares	——	**green**
rectangles	——	**yellow**
circles	——	**red**
triangles	——	**blue**

Name _____

"Squaring" Off

Square dancing is a kind of folk dancing. The name of the dance comes from the shape the group of dancers form when they begin the dance – a square. As they dance, they form other shapes.

Look at the shapes and answer the questions.

How many ☐ 's can you find?

_____

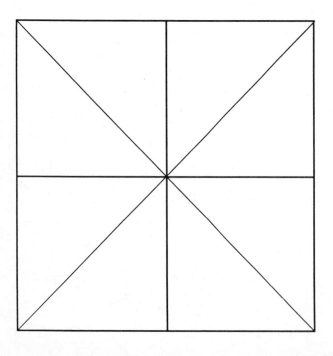

One pattern the dancers form is called "a star." Each person puts one arm into the middle of the square. The square is cut into △ 's.

How many △ 's can you find?

_____

Name _____

Rainbow-Colored Numbers

Color: 1's—red
       2's—blue
       3's—yellow
       4's—green
       5's—orange

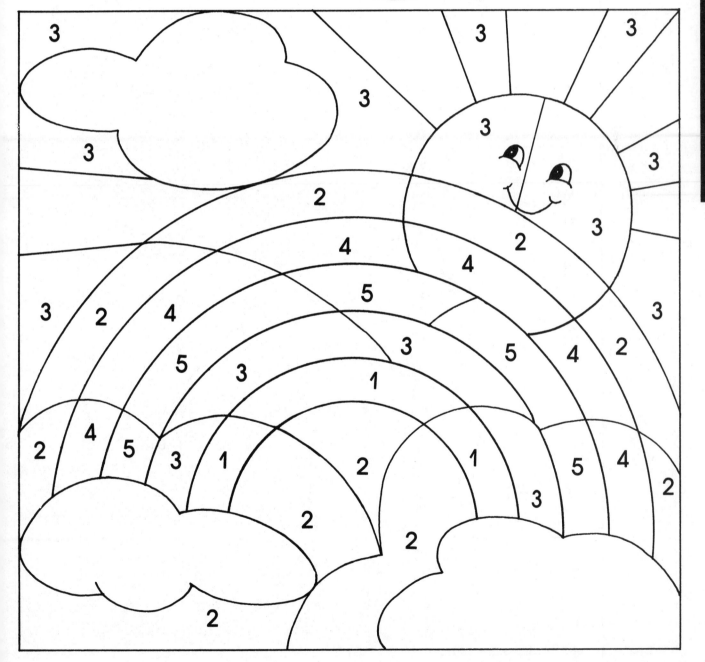

Name _____

One Beautiful Butterfly

Color: 6's—purple
7's—yellow
8's—black
9's—orange
10's—brown

Name _____

Clown Count

 the 🎈's:

1 - blue   2 - orange   3 - yellow   4 - green

                5 - purple   6 - brown

7 - red   8 - black   9 - blue   10 - purple

Color clown, too!

Name _____

Wintry Ride

Count each set of bears. Draw a line from each set to the sled that has the correct number.

Name _____

Pack a Snack

Count each set of sandwiches. Draw a line from each set to the backpack that has the correct number.

Name _____

Sheepish Shepherd

Count the sheep on each hill. Then write that number on each tree.

Name _____

Number Express

Number the train.

Draw a line from the word to the number.

seven	1
two	8
five	3
nine	4
six	7
four	5
one	6
three	2
eight	9

Color train cars.　　one-**red**　　three-**green**　　five-**orange**

two-**blue**　　four-**yellow**　　six-**brown**

Name _____

Beach Blanket Numbers
Count. Use code to color answers.

1—blue   4—red   7—purple
2—yellow 5—orange 8—gray
3—green   6—brown 9—black

Name _____

School Scene

How many?

Name _____

Take an Animal Count!

Count the zoo animals in each box. Match the number to the correct number word by drawing a line to it. One is done for you.

four

eight

one

ten

seven

two

six

three

nine

five

Name _____

Connect the Dots

Join the dots in order.
Color the surprise.

•1
•3
•2
20 •

15 •

•16
14 •
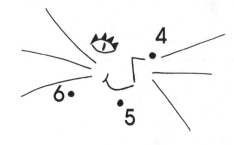
•4
6 •
5

•19

•7

•8

•17
13 •
•18

12 •
11 •
•9
10 •

Name _____

More Dot-to-Dot Fun

Connect the dots.

Name _____

Happy Hikers

Hike your way to camp. Trace a path through the maze by counting from 1 to 10 in the correct order. Color the picture.

Daily Learning Drills Grade 1

Name _____

Two for the Pool

Counting by 2's, write the numbers to 50 in the waterdrops. Start at the top of the slide and go down.

Name _____

I'm Counting on You

Write and count by 2's.

Write and count by 5's.

MATH

Connect the dots by 2's.

Connect the dots by 5's.

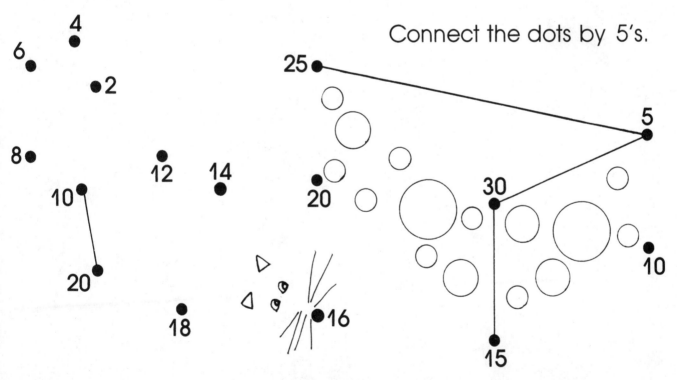

Name _____

Count the Cookie Clues

Find out what holds something crumbly, but good! Counting by 5's, connect the dots in order. Start with 5. Color the picture.

Name _____

Desert Trek

As you count by 10's, color each canteen with the number you say to lead the camel to the watering hole.

Daily Learning Drills Grade 1

Name _____

Caterpillar Count

Circle numbers
counting by twos.

1, ②, 3, 4, 5, 6, 7,
8, 9, 10, 11, 12, 13,
14, 15, 16, 17, 18, 19,
20, 21, 22, 23, 24

Count by 2's.

2 , 4 , ____ , ____ , ____ , ____ , ____ , ____

Put △ around
numbers counting
by fives.

1, 2, 3, 4, △5△ 6, 7, 8, 9,
10, 11, 12, 13, 14, 15, 16,
17, 18, 19, 20, 21, 22,
23, 24, 25, 26, 27,
28, 29, 30, 31, 32, 33,
34, 35, 36, 37, 38, 39, 40

Count by 5's.

5 , 10 , ____ , ____ , ____ , ____ , ____ , ____

Put □ around
numbers counting
by 10's.

1, 2, 3, 4, 5, 6, 7, 8, 9, [10,] 11,
12, 13, 14, 15, 16, 17, 18, 19,
20, 21, 22, 23, 24, 25, 26,
27, 28, 29, 30, 31, 32, 33

Count by 10's.

10 , ____ , ____ , ____ , ____ , ____ , ____ , ____

Name _____

Largest and Smallest

In the shapes, circle the smallest number.

Draw a square around the largest number.

Name _____

Barking Up a Tree

Use counters. Trace or draw each set you make. Then, write how many in all.

How many? How many more? How many in all?

| 3 | + | 2 | = | ____ |

| 2 | + | 1 | = | ____ |

| 4 | + | 3 | = | ____ |

| 1 | + | 6 | = | ____ |

Think of a story for this picture. Write how many in all.

| ____ in all |

Name _____

How Many in All?

$2 + 2 = 4$

$$\begin{array}{r} 2 \\ + 2 \\ \hline 4 \end{array}$$

Write an addition sentence and a vertical fact for each picture story. Find how many in all.

$$\begin{array}{r} \underline{} \\ + \underline{} \\ \hline \end{array}$$

___ + ___ = ___

$$\begin{array}{r} \underline{} \\ + \underline{} \\ \hline \end{array}$$

___ + ___ = ___

$$\begin{array}{r} \underline{} \\ + \underline{} \\ \hline \end{array}$$

___ + ___ = ___

$$\begin{array}{r} \underline{} \\ + \underline{} \\ \hline \end{array}$$

___ + ___ = ___

$$\begin{array}{r} \underline{} \\ + \underline{} \\ \hline \end{array}$$

___ + ___ = ___

$$\begin{array}{r} \underline{} \\ + \underline{} \\ \hline \end{array}$$

___ + ___ = ___

Daily Learning Drills Grade 1

MATH

Name _____

Addition Using Counters

| Example | $2 + 1 = \underline{\ ?\ }$ |

Use counters to add.

Put in 2.	Put in 1 more.

How many counters are there in all? __3__

So, $2 + 1 = \underline{3}$. The number that tells how many in all is called the **sum**. The sum of 2 + 1 is 3.

Use counters to find each sum.

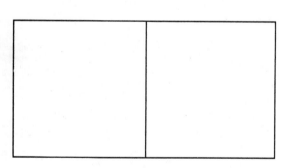

$2 + 4 = \underline{\ \ \ }$

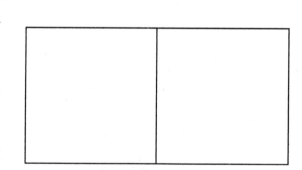

$5 + 2 = \underline{\ \ \ }$

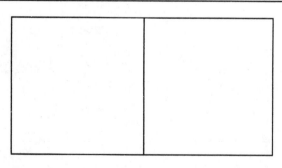

$3 + 3 = \underline{\ \ \ }$

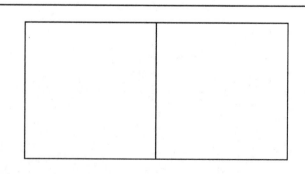

$3 + 4 = \underline{\ \ \ }$

Name _____

Prehistoric Picture Problems

Circle the picture which matches the number sentence.

1. $1 + 2 = 3$

or

2. $2 + 3 = 5$

or

3. $4 + 2 = 6$

or

4. $5 + 1 = 6$

or

5. $3 + 4 = 7$

or

6. $6 + 1 = 7$

or

Name _____

Alien Problems

Look at the pictures and finish the number sentences.

1.

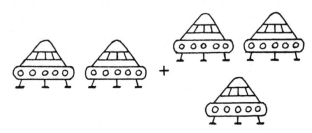

$$2 + 3 = \underline{}$$

2.

$$1 + 7 = \underline{}$$

3.

$$4 + 3 = \underline{}$$

4.

$$5 + 0 = \underline{}$$

5.

$$3 + 3 = \underline{}$$

6.

$$4 + 5 = \underline{}$$

Name _____

Bear Necessities: How Many More Are Needed?

Draw in the missing pictures and finish the number sentences.

1.

$1 + \underline{2} = 3$

2.

$3 + \underline{} = 5$

3.

$5 + \underline{} = 8$

4.

$3 + \underline{} = 6$

5.

$2 + \underline{} = 7$

6.

$4 + \underline{} = 5$

Name _____

The Missing Chickens

Draw in the missing pictures and finish the number sentences.

1.

____1____ + 2 = 3

2.

_____ + 3 = 6

3.

5 + _____ = 7

4.

_____ + 3 = 5

5.

_____ + 4 = 8

6.

7 + _____ = 8

Name _____

How Many Robots in All?

Look at the pictures and finish the number sentences.

1.

How many 's are there in all?

$$2 + 4 = \underline{6}$$

2.

How many 's are there in all?

$$3 + 5 = \underline{\hspace{2cm}}$$

3.

How many 's are there in all?

$$4 + 3 = \underline{\hspace{2cm}}$$

4.

How many 's are there in all?

$$4 + 1 = \underline{\hspace{2cm}}$$

5.

How many 's are there in all?

$$2 + 5 = \underline{\hspace{2cm}}$$

6.

How many 's are there in all?

$$4 + 4 = \underline{\hspace{2cm}}$$

MATH

Name _____

How Many Rabbits?

Look at the pictures and finish the number sentences.

1.

How many 's are there in all?

$$1 + 1 = \underline{2}$$

2.

How many 's are there in all?

$$3 + 6 = \underline{}$$

3.

How many 's are there in all?

$$6 + 1 = \underline{}$$

4.

How many 's are there in all?

$$3 + 4 = \underline{}$$

5.

How many 's are there in all?

$$4 + 5 = \underline{}$$

6.

How many 's are there in all?

$$2 + 3 = \underline{}$$

Name _____

Bee Addition

 $+$ $=$ 3 + 1 =

Add. Use code to color each bee.   2—red   4—blue
3—yellow   5—green

 1 + 2 = _____

 2 + 3 = _____

 3 + 2 = _____

 3 + 1 = _____

 1 + 1 = _____

 2 + 2 = _____

 2 + 1 = _____

 1 + 3 = _____

Name _____

Lumberjack Facts

Add.

If the answer equals **1**, color the space **red**.
If the answer equals **2**, color the space **yellow**.
If the answer equals **3**, color the space **black**.
If the answer equals **4**, color the space **blue**.
If the answer equals **5**, color the space **brown**.
If the answer equals **6**, color the space **green**.

Name _____

Creature Count

5 + 1 = 6

4 + 6 =   1 + 9 =

7 + 1 =   7 + 3 =

5 + 2 =   6 + 1 =

8 + 2 =   3 + 5 =

6 + 3 =   6 + 2 =

4 + 5 =   1 + 7 =

MATH

Name _____

Beary Good

Put counters on each bear to show the addition. Write the sums.

3 + 2 = ___   5 + 0 = ___   1 + 6 = ___   4 + 2 = ___

$$\begin{array}{r} 6 \\ +\ 1 \\ \hline \end{array} \qquad \begin{array}{r} 3 \\ +\ 4 \\ \hline \end{array} \qquad \begin{array}{r} 2 \\ +\ 3 \\ \hline \end{array} \qquad \begin{array}{r} 5 \\ +\ 2 \\ \hline \end{array} \qquad \begin{array}{r} 7 \\ +\ 1 \\ \hline \end{array} \qquad \begin{array}{r} 0 \\ +\ 2 \\ \hline \end{array}$$

$$\begin{array}{r} 8 \\ +\ 0 \\ \hline \end{array} \qquad \begin{array}{r} 4 \\ +\ 5 \\ \hline \end{array} \qquad \begin{array}{r} 3 \\ +\ 6 \\ \hline \end{array} \qquad \begin{array}{r} 2 \\ +\ 6 \\ \hline \end{array} \qquad \begin{array}{r} 3 \\ +\ 5 \\ \hline \end{array} \qquad \begin{array}{r} 6 \\ +\ 2 \\ \hline \end{array}$$

Name _____

Animal Addition

4	+	7	=	11

Add.

3 + 9 = __12__

6 + 7 = _____

6 + 5 = _____

5 + 7 = _____

4 + 9 = _____

9 + 6 = _____

7 + 7 = _____

7 + 8 = _____

6 + 8 = _____

Daily Learning Drills Grade 1

Name _____

Add the Apples

Match.

8 + 2   15

9 + 6   4

2 + 2   10

1 + 2   11

6 + 7   3

5 + 6   13

6 + 2   8

1 + 1   6

1 + 5   2

3 + 2   10

6 + 8   14

5 + 5   5

6 + 6   12

6 + 3   9

3 + 4   7

7 + 2   15

6 + 9   9

12 + 1   13

10 + 1   14

9 + 5   8

7 + 1   11

Name _____

What's the Difference?

| Example | $5 - 2 = \underline{?}$ |

Use counters to subtract.

Put in 5. Take away 2.

How many counters are left? _3_

So, $5 - 2 = 3$. The number that tells how many are left is called the **difference**. The difference of $5 - 2$ is 3.

Use counters to find each difference.

$6 - 3 = \underline{\ \ }$

$5 - 1 = \underline{\ \ }$

$5 - 3 = \underline{\ \ }$

$4 - 2 = \underline{\ \ }$

MATH

Daily Learning Drills Grade 1

Name _____

Counting Kittens

Use counters. Make a set, then take away. Write how many are left.

_____ are left.

Put in 4. Take away 1.

_____ are left.

Put in 5. Take away 2.

_____ are left.

Put in 6. Take away 1.

_____ are left.

Put in 7. Take away 3.

Think of a story for this picture. Write how many are left.

_____ are left.

Name _____

Transportation Problems

Circle the picture which matches the number sentence. Then finish the number sentence.

1.

$$4 - 1 = \text{\_\_\_\_}$$

2.
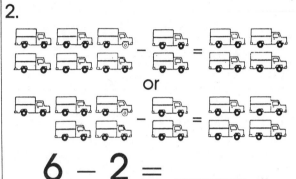

$$6 - 2 = \text{\_\_\_\_}$$

3.

$$5 - 3 = \text{\_\_\_\_}$$

4.

$$7 - 3 = \text{\_\_\_\_}$$

5.

$$5 - 2 = \text{\_\_\_\_}$$

6.

$$7 - 5 = \text{\_\_\_\_}$$

Name _____

Sea Creature Subtraction

Look at the pictures and finish the number sentences.

1.

How many 's are left?

$$4 - 4 = 0$$

2.

How many 's are left?

$$6 - 2 = \underline{\hspace{2cm}}$$

3.

How many 's are left?

$$7 - 3 = \underline{\hspace{2cm}}$$

4.

How many 's are left?

$$6 - 5 = \underline{\hspace{2cm}}$$

5.

How many 's are left?

$$8 - 3 = \underline{\hspace{2cm}}$$

6.

How many 's are left?

$$5 - 2 = \underline{\hspace{2cm}}$$

Name _____

Nutty Subtraction

Count the nuts.
Write answer on blank.
Circle problems with same answer.

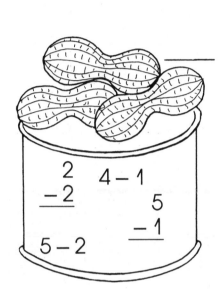

$$\begin{array}{r} 2 \\ -2 \\ \hline \end{array}$$ $4 - 1$

$$\begin{array}{r} 5 \\ -1 \\ \hline \end{array}$$

$5 - 2$

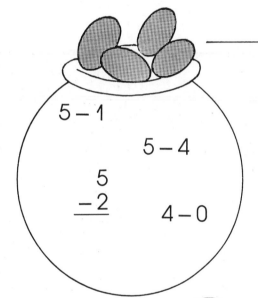

$5 - 1$

$5 - 4$

$$\begin{array}{r} 5 \\ -2 \\ \hline \end{array}$$

$4 - 0$

$4 - 2$

$$\begin{array}{r} 4 \\ -1 \\ \hline \end{array}$$ $$\begin{array}{r} 5 \\ -3 \\ \hline \end{array}$$

$3 - 1$

$5 - 0$ $$\begin{array}{r} 2 \\ -2 \\ \hline \end{array}$$

$$\begin{array}{r} 5 \\ -1 \\ \hline \end{array}$$ $$\begin{array}{r} 4 \\ -3 \\ \hline \end{array}$$

Daily Learning Drills Grade 1

Name _____

Robins and Worms

$$3 - 2 = 1$$

$$\begin{array}{r} 3 \\ -2 \\ \hline 1 \end{array}$$

$5 - 1 = $ _____ $3 - 1 = $ _____ $5 - 2 = $ _____

$4 - 1 = $ _____ $2 - 1 = $ _____ $4 - 2 = $ _____

$3 - 2 = $ _____ $4 - 3 = $ _____ $5 - 3 = $ _____

Subtract. Use code to color worms. **1—red** **3—yellow**
2—orange **4—brown**

$5 - 1 = \bigcirc$
$$\begin{array}{r} 5 \\ -1 \\ \hline \end{array}$$
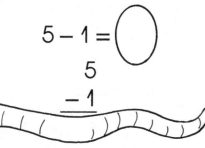

$4 - 2 = \bigcirc$
$$\begin{array}{r} 4 \\ -2 \\ \hline \end{array}$$

$5 - 2 = \bigcirc$
$$\begin{array}{r} 5 \\ -2 \\ \hline \end{array}$$

$3 - 1 = \bigcirc$
$$\begin{array}{r} 3 \\ -1 \\ \hline \end{array}$$
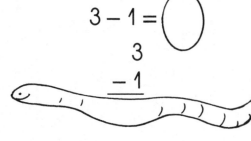

$4 - 3 = \bigcirc$
$$\begin{array}{r} 4 \\ -3 \\ \hline \end{array}$$

$5 - 3 = \bigcirc$
$$\begin{array}{r} 5 \\ -3 \\ \hline \end{array}$$
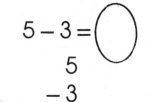

$2 - 1 = \bigcirc$
$$\begin{array}{r} 2 \\ -1 \\ \hline \end{array}$$

$4 - 1 = \bigcirc$
$$\begin{array}{r} 4 \\ -1 \\ \hline \end{array}$$

$3 - 2 = \bigcirc$
$$\begin{array}{r} 3 \\ -2 \\ \hline \end{array}$$

Name _____

"Berry" Tasty

Subtract.

If the answer is **0**, color the space **green**.

If the answer is **1**, color the space **brown**.

If the answer is **2**, color the space **blue**.

If the answer is **3**, color the space **purple**.

If the answer is **4**, color the space **black**.

If the answer is **5**, color the space **pink**.

MATH

Name _____

Bubbly Baths

Subtract. Write each answer on the rubber duck.

Name _____

Fewer Fruits

$9 - 2 = 7$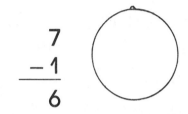

$\begin{array}{r} 7 \\ -1 \\ \hline 6 \end{array}$

Subtract. Use code to color.

6—orange   9—green
7—red   10—purple
8—yellow

$11 - 1 =$	$\begin{array}{r} 9 \\ -1 \\ \hline \end{array}$	$8 - 1 =$
$10 - 4 =$	$\begin{array}{r} 9 \\ -2 \\ \hline \end{array}$ 	$\begin{array}{r} 10 \\ -1 \\ \hline \end{array}$
$10 - 2 =$	$11 - 2 =$	$\begin{array}{r} 10 \\ -3 \\ \hline \end{array}$ 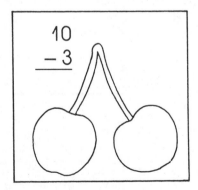

Name _____

Sweet Treats

Count the candy.
Write number on blank.
Circle problems with same answer.

_____

$$9 - 3 \qquad 7 - 1$$
$$\begin{array}{r} 8 \\ -2 \end{array} \qquad \begin{array}{r} 9 \\ -2 \end{array}$$

_____

$$10 - 1$$
$$\qquad 10 - 4$$
$$\begin{array}{r} 11 \\ -2 \end{array} \qquad \begin{array}{r} 9 \\ -1 \end{array}$$

$$\begin{array}{r} 10 \\ -4 \end{array}$$
$$9 - 2 \qquad \begin{array}{r} 8 \\ -1 \end{array} \qquad 10 - 3$$

$$\begin{array}{r} 10 \\ -4 \end{array} \quad 7 - 2 \quad \begin{array}{r} 8 \\ -2 \end{array}$$
$$8 - 2$$

_____

_____

$$\begin{array}{r} 9 \\ -4 \end{array} \qquad 10 - 2$$
$$10 - 1 \qquad \begin{array}{r} 9 \\ -1 \end{array}$$

Name _____

A Whale of a Job!

For each problem, put the number of counters needed in the water, then take away by sliding the numbers into the whale's mouth. Then, count how many counters are left in the water to find the difference.

$$\begin{array}{r} 7 \\ -\ 3 \\ \hline \end{array} \qquad \begin{array}{r} 9 \\ -\ 2 \\ \hline \end{array} \qquad \begin{array}{r} 6 \\ -\ 4 \\ \hline \end{array} \qquad \begin{array}{r} 5 \\ -\ 2 \\ \hline \end{array} \qquad \begin{array}{r} 8 \\ -\ 3 \\ \hline \end{array}$$

$$\begin{array}{r} 9 \\ -\ 3 \\ \hline \end{array} \qquad \begin{array}{r} 6 \\ -\ 3 \\ \hline \end{array} \qquad \begin{array}{r} 7 \\ -\ 5 \\ \hline \end{array} \qquad \begin{array}{r} 8 \\ -\ 2 \\ \hline \end{array} \qquad \begin{array}{r} 5 \\ -\ 1 \\ \hline \end{array}$$

8 − 4 = _____   6 − 2 = _____   7 − 4 = _____

Name _____

Hop Along Numbers

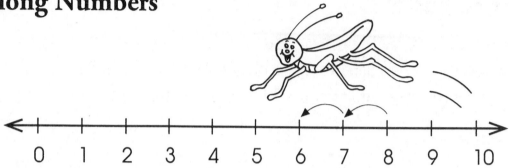

Use the number line to **count back**.

8, _7_ , _6_ | 6, ___ , ___

5, ___ , ___ | 7, ___ , ___ , ___

Use the number line to count back to find each difference.

Example: $9 - 2 =$ _?_ Start with 9. Count back 2.

9, ___ , ___ $9 - 2 =$ ___

7 − 3 = ___

7, ___ , ___

6 − 2 = ___

6, ___ , ___

8 − 1 = ___

8, ___

7 − 2 = ___

7, ___ , ___

Name _____

Crayon Count

Count crayons. Write number on blank.
Circle problems that name answer.

11
_____

13 − 2 =   14
            − 3

15 − 4 =
   13
   − 2   15 − 5 =

      12 − 1 =

_____

12   13 − 3 =
− 1

               15
12 − 2 =   − 5
13   11
− 3   − 1

_____

15 − 2 =   14
               − 1
    14
    − 2

14 − 1 =   15
               − 2
15 − 3 =

_____

14   15 − 4 =
− 2
    13
    − 1   15
              − 3
14 − 2 =
14 − 4 =

_____

15 − 1 =
    12
    − 1   13 − 1 =

                15
10 − 1 =   − 1

12 − 2 =

Name _____

Turtle Math—Take It Slow

Color answer:
2—red
3—blue
4—yellow
5—green

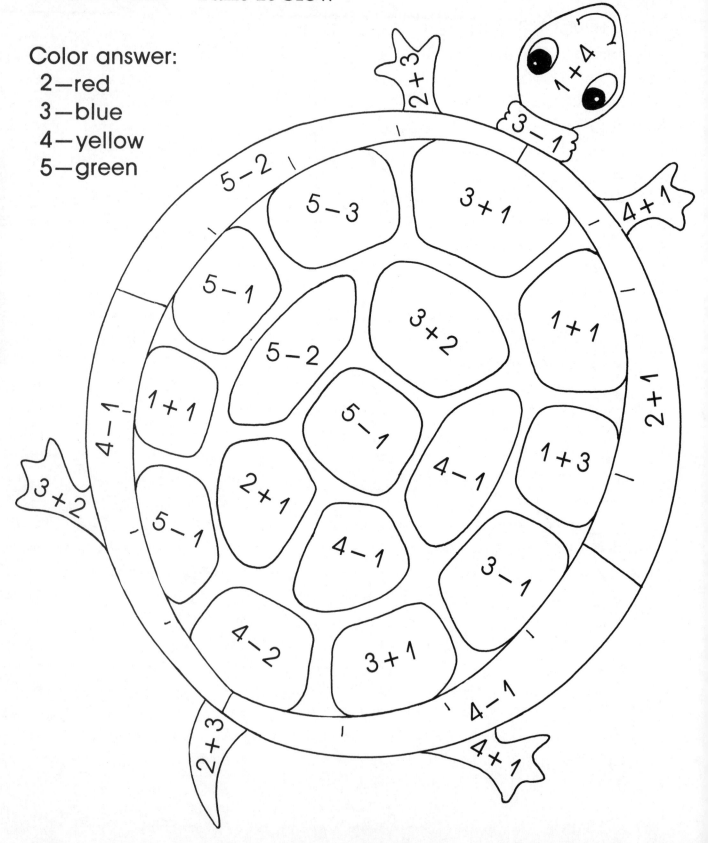

Name _____

It's Show Time

It's time for Packy and Dermit to perform. Look at the problems.

Write **+** or **−** on each peanut to make the problem correct. Then trace a path from peanut to peanut, connecting each elephant to the correct stool. For Packy, connect all of the **+** problems. For Dermit, connect all of the **−** problems.

3 ◯ 2 = 5

10 ◯ 8 = 2

Packy

Dermit

2 ◯ 6 = 8

7 ◯ 3 = 4

8 ◯ 2 = 6

5 ◯ 4 = 9

9 ◯ 4 = 5

5 ◯ 5 = 10

10 ◯ 3 = 7

3 ◯ 3 = 0

9 ◯ 1 = 10

7 ◯ 5 = 2

6 ◯ 4 = 10

6 ◯ 3 = 3

5 ◯ 2 = 7

5 ◯ 3 = 8

2 ◯ 7 = 9

Daily Learning Drills Grade 1

Name _____

Puppy Problems

Look at the pictures and finish the number sentences.

1. $5 \bigodot 6 = \underline{11}$

2. $11 \bigcirc 4 = \underline{\hspace{2cm}}$

3. $12 \bigcirc 7 = \underline{\hspace{2cm}}$

4. $7 \bigcirc 6 = \underline{\hspace{2cm}}$

5. $5 \bigcirc 5 = \underline{\hspace{2cm}}$

6. $8 \bigcirc 6 = \underline{\hspace{2cm}}$

Name _____

Calling All Cats

Look at the pictures and finish the number sentences.

1.
How many 🐱's are there in all?

$7 \oplus 4 = \underline{11}$

2.
How many 🐱's are there in all?

$6 \bigcirc 8 = \underline{}$

3.
How many 🐱's are there in all?

$11 \bigcirc 2 = \underline{}$

4.
How many 🐱's are left?

$13 \bigcirc 7 = \underline{}$

5.
How many 🐱's are left?

$9 \bigcirc 6 = \underline{}$

6.
How many 🐱's are left?

$12 \bigcirc 8 = \underline{}$

Name _____

What Was the Question?

Draw a line under the question that matches the picture. Then finish the number sentence.

1.

How many 🐸's are there in all?
How many 🐸's are left?

$11 - 7 = \underline{4}$

2.

How many 🐢's are there in all?
How many 🐢's are left?

$4 + 5 = \underline{}$

3.

How many 🍄's are there in all?
How many 🍄's are left?

$8 - 3 = \underline{}$

4.

How many 🍄's are there in all?
How many 🍄's are left?

$10 - 4 = \underline{}$

5.

How many 🐌's are there in all?
How many 🐌's are left?

$5 + 6 = \underline{}$

6.

How many 🐸's are there in all?
How many 🐸's are left?

$8 + 4 = \underline{}$

Name _____

Sunny Day Delight

Draw a line under the question that matches the picture.
Then finish the number sentence.

1.

How many 🍦's are there in all?
How many 🍦's are left?

$6 + 6 = \underline{12}$

2.

How many 🍦's are there in all?
How many 🍦's are left?

$13 - 4 = \underline{\hspace{1cm}}$

3.

How many 🍦's are there in all?
How many 🍦's are left?

$9 + 5 = \underline{\hspace{1cm}}$

4.

How many 🍦's are there in all?
How many 🍦's are left?

$13 - 5 = \underline{\hspace{1cm}}$

5.

How many 🍦's are there in all?
How many 🍦's are left?

$7 + 7 = \underline{\hspace{1cm}}$

6.

How many 🍦's are there in all?
How many 🍦's are left?

$9 - 5 = \underline{\hspace{1cm}}$

MATH

Name _____

Fishing for Answers

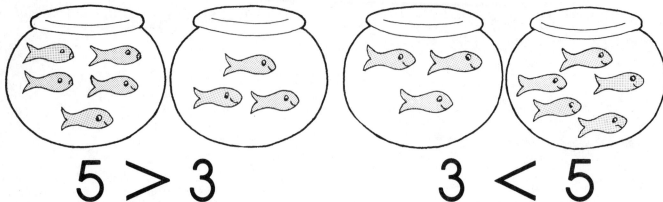

5 > 3

5 is **greater than** 3.

3 < 5

3 is **less than** 5.

Fill in number line.

1	2			6				

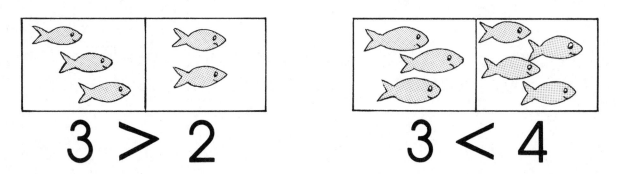

3 > 2

3 < 4

Write > or <. Use number line to help you.

5 _____ 2   1 _____ 7   1 _____ 9   8 _____ 5

3 _____ 4   9 _____ 3   8 _____ 7   2 _____ 4

6 _____ 5   5 _____ 3   5 _____ 7   3 _____ 5

7 _____ 3   7 _____ 6   2 _____ 8   4 _____ 2

Name _____

Split in Two

How many
equal parts? _____

  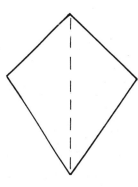

Color shapes with 2 equal parts.

  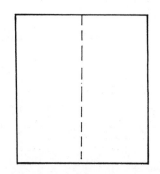

MATH

Name _____

Thirds

How many equal parts? __3__

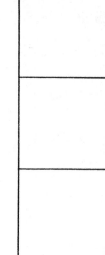

Color shapes with 3 equal parts.

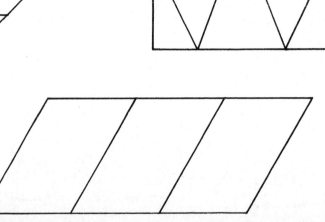

Name _____

Fourths

How many equal parts? _____

Color shapes with 4 equal parts.

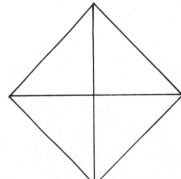

Name _____

Fractions Review

How many equal parts?

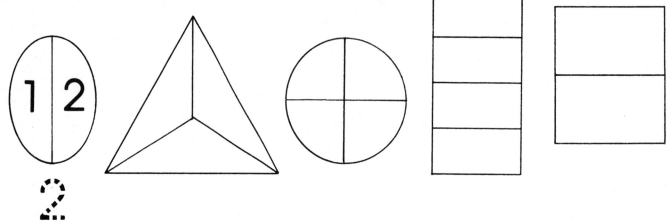

Color shapes with 2 equal parts red,
3 parts blue and 4 parts green.

Name _____

A Race!

first
second
third
fourth
fifth
sixth
seventh

Write the correct word to tell where each runner placed in the race.

1. _____

2. _____

3. _____

4. _____

5. _____

6. _____

7. _____

Flip Fun! Draw a prize you would like to receive for winning a race.

Name _____

Flags First

Color the **ninth** flag red.
Write **O** on the **second** flag.
Color the **eighth** flag blue.
Write **D** on the **fourth** flag.
Color the **sixth** flag yellow.
Write **G** on the **first** flag.
Color the **tenth** flag purple.
Write **O** on the **third** flag.
Color the **seventh** flag green.
Color the **fifth** flag orange.

Name _____

Balls of All Kinds

Color second
ball brown.

Color sixth
ball yellow.

Color fourth
ball orange.

Color first
ball black.

Color third
ball blue.

Color fifth
ball green.

Color seventh
ball purple.

Color eighth
ball pink.

Daily Learning Drills Grade 1

MATH

Name _____

Henny Penny

1¢ 1 penny
      1 cent

How much money?

Example

1¢ 1¢ 1¢   1¢ 1¢ 1¢ 1¢
1¢ 1¢ = 5 ¢   1¢ 1¢ = ☐ ¢

1¢ 1¢ = ☐ ¢   1¢ 1¢ 1¢ = ☐ ¢

1¢ 1¢ 1¢   1¢ 1¢ 1¢ 1¢
1¢ = ☐ ¢   1¢ 1¢ 1¢ 1¢ = ☐ ¢

1¢ 1¢ 1¢ 1¢ 1¢ 1¢ 1¢ = ☐ ¢

Name _____

Penny Pinchers

Draw a line from the pennies to the right numbers.

Example

Daily Learning Drills Grade 1

MATH

Name _____

Nickel Pickles

 5 cents
1 nickel

How much money?

$= \boxed{15} ¢$

Count __5__ , __10__ , __15__

$= \boxed{} ¢$

Count ____ , ____

$= \boxed{} ¢$

Count ____ , ____ , ____

$= \boxed{} ¢$

Count ____ , ____ , ____ , ____

____ , ____

$= \boxed{} ¢$

Count ____ , ____ , ____ , ____

$= \boxed{} ¢$

Count ____ , ____ , ____

____ , ____ , ____

Name _____

Five Hive

How much money is in each hive?

5¢
5¢
5¢
5¢   **20** ¢

5¢
5¢
5¢
5¢
5¢   _____ ¢

5¢
5¢   _____ ¢

5¢
5¢
5¢
5¢
5¢
5¢   _____ ¢

5¢
5¢
5¢   _____ ¢

5¢   _____ ¢

5¢
5¢
5¢
5¢
5¢
5¢
5¢   _____ ¢

5¢
5¢
5¢
5¢
5¢
5¢
5¢
5¢   _____ ¢

5¢
5¢
5¢
5¢
5¢
5¢
5¢
5¢   _____ ¢

MATH

Daily Learning Drills Grade 1

Name _____

Money Bunnies

Count the coins. Write the amount under each bunny's carrot.

7¢

Name _____

Cent-erpillars

Count the coins on each "cent"erpillar.

__17__ ¢

_____ ¢

_____ ¢

_____ ¢

_____ ¢

_____ ¢

_____ ¢

_____ ¢

_____ ¢

_____ ¢

Daily Learning Drills Grade 1

Name _____

Marching Dimes

Come march with my dime friends and me!

Count by 10's.

___10___ ¢   _____   _____

_____   _____   _____   _____

Count by 10's. Write the number. Make a circle around the group which is **more**.

___30___ ¢   ___10___ ¢

_____ ¢   _____ ¢

_____ ¢   _____ ¢

Name _____

Dime Climbs

Climb the trees and count the money.
Write the answer under each tree.

33¢ _____

_____

_____

_____

_____

_____

_____

_____

_____

MATH

Name _____

Buy and Buy

Circle the coins to equal the right amount.

Example

Name _____

Sir Circle Counts Coins!

Count the coins. Circle the set with more money.

Example

12¢ _____ 21¢ _____

_____ _____

_____ _____

_____ _____

_____ _____

_____ _____

_____ _____

_____ _____

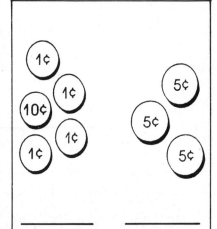

_____ _____

MATH

Name _____

Watch the Time

Show the class how to put numbers on the watch and draw watch hands.
Students then color and cut out the watch. Tape it to fit the wrist.

1 2 3
4 5 6
7 8 9
10 11 12

Name _____

Hickory Dickory Dock

What time is it?

___o'clock   ___o'clock   ___o'clock

___o'clock   ___o'clock   ___o'clock

___o'clock   ___o'clock   ___o'clock

___o'clock   ___o'clock   ___o'clock

    Daily Learning Drills Grade 1

Name _____

Here's the Scoop!

Draw the hour hand on each clock.

8 o'clock

4 o'clock

2 o'clock

6 o'clock

11 o'clock

3 o'clock

1 o'clock

5 o'clock

7 o'clock

Name _____

Timely News

Cut out the newspapers at the bottom of the page. Paste each newspaper below the correct clock.

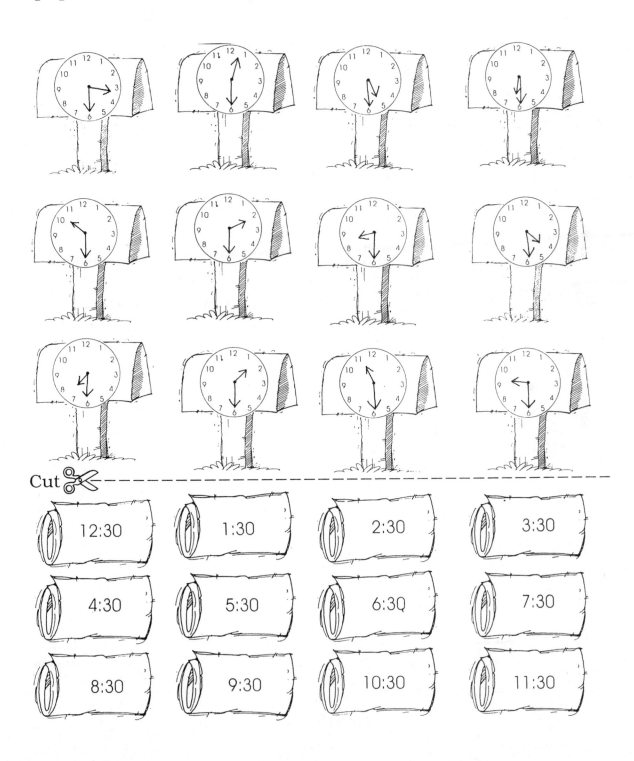

Cut ✂ --

12:30	1:30	2:30	3:30
4:30	5:30	6:30	7:30
8:30	9:30	10:30	11:30

Daily Learning Drills Grade 1

Name _____

Who "Nose" These Times?

Write the time under each clock.
Color the noses.

4:00   4:30

Name _____

Sock Clocks

Draw the hands on the sock clocks.

1:30   7:00   4:30

10:00   3:30   9:30

4:00   2:30   6:00

Name _____

It's Time to Eat!

Follow the directions below the clock.

1. Draw a yellow banana at 7:00.
2. Draw a hamburger at 12:00.
3. Draw a red apple at 10:00.
4. Draw a fried egg at 6:00.
5. Draw a hot dog at 11:00.
6. Draw an orange carrot at 1:00.
7. Draw a piece of pizza at 5:00.
8. Draw a donut at 9:00.
9. Draw an ice cream cone with three flavors at 2:00.
10. Draw an ear of corn at 4:00.
11. Draw a chicken leg at 8:00.
12. Draw your favorite food at 3:00.

Name _____

What a Day!

The camp director needs help planning activities for tomorrow afternoon. Read the list carefully. Then use the times to number the activities in the order they will happen.

____ 5:30 p.m. Supper
____ 4:30 p.m. Crafts
____ 1:30 p.m. Baseball game
____ 3:00 p.m. Swimming
____ 2:30 p.m. Water Safety
____ 1:00 p.m. Walk in the woods
____ 6:30 p.m. Boating
____ 12:30 p.m. First Aid Lesson
____ 12:00 noon Lunch
____ 7:30 p.m. Campfire

Which activity would you most enjoy doing? Why?

_____

_____

_____

Which activity would you least enjoy doing? Why?

_____

_____

Name _____

It's About Time

There are many ways we measure time. A year is made of 365 days. A week has seven days. A day has 24 hours. An hour is made of 60 minutes. A minute is made of 60 seconds. A second goes very quickly. Can you blink your eyes in one second?

| day | year | minute | week | hour |

Write.

1 ↓ 365 days make a y __ __ __.

2 → Seven days make a w __ __ __.

3 → 24 hours make a d __ __.

4 → 60 minutes make an h __ __ __.

5 ↓ 60 seconds make a m __ __ __ __ __.

Write the answers in the puzzle above.

Check.

The words in the puzzle tell about ☐ money. ☐ time.

• Write a list of what you can do in **two** minutes.

Name _____

Fun Days

There are seven days in a week. Saturday and Sunday are the weekend days. You go to school the other five days. Which day do you like best?

 How many days are in a week?

six   seven   ten

Which two days make a weekend?

| Saturday |
| Thursday |
| Sunday |

_____
- - - - - - - - - - - -
_____
- - - - - - - - - - - -
_____

 the five days you go to school.

• Draw and color what you do on a weekend.

Name _____

Hmm, What Month Is It?

There are twelve months in a year. The first month is January. The last month is December. Some months have 31 days. Some months have 30 days. February is the shortest month with 28 days. Can you name the months of the year?

☐ April

☐ October

☐ December   ☐ July

☐ March   [1] January

☐ May

☐ September

☐ June

☐ February

☐ August

☐ November

Check.

How many months are in a year?

☐ five
☐ nine
☐ twelve

Write.

_____   _____
          first month   last month

Circle.

Yes or No

Some months have 30 days.	Yes	No
Some months have 31 days.	Yes	No
February is the longest month.	Yes	No
February has 28 days.	Yes	No

Write **1-12** in the ☐'s to put the months in order.

• Write the names of the twelve months in the correct order.

Name _____

How Did You Do That?

You use many parts of your body to do even the simplest activities.

Read each activity and write the body parts you would use to do that activity.

Activities:

1. read a book

   _____
   _____

2. talk to your friend on the phone

   _____
   _____

3. put on your hat

   _____
   _____

4. blow out the candles on a cake

   _____
   _____

5. eat an ice-cream cone

   _____
   _____

6. ride a bike to school

   _____
   _____

Name _____

Body Buddies

Arrange the numbers to print a word that is part of your body. Then color each part.

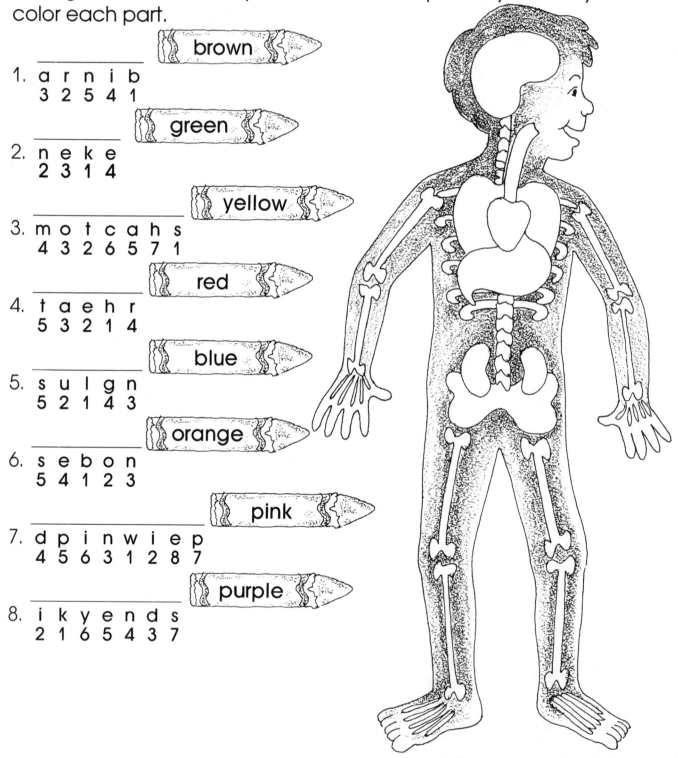

_____ brown

1. a r n i b
   3 2 5 4 1

_____ green

2. n e k e
   2 3 1 4

_____ yellow

3. m o t c a h s
   4 3 2 6 5 7 1

_____ red

4. t a e h r
   5 3 2 1 4

_____ blue

5. s u l g n
   5 2 1 4 3

_____ orange

6. s e b o n
   5 4 1 2 3

_____ pink

7. d p i n w i e p
   4 5 6 3 1 2 8 7

_____ purple

8. i k y e n d s
   2 1 6 5 4 3 7

Name _____

It Makes Sense to Me

Our five senses help us understand and make "sense" of our world. Look at each group of pictures. Decide which sense (**see, hear, smell, taste, or feel**) is used for most items in each group of pictures. Write the sense on the line below each group. Then put an **X** on the one picture that does not belong in each group.

SCIENCE

Name _____

Outfitted for Health

Read the phrases in the Word Bank. Write only the **good** health habits on the lines.

Word Bank	Take a bath.	Eat a lot of sweets	Stay up all night.
	Drink water.	Get plenty of sleep.	Keep cuts clean.
	Sit all day.	Never wash your hands.	Brush your teeth.
	Exercise.	Eat healthy foods.	

 1. _____

 2. _____

 3. _____

 4. _____

 5. _____

6. _____

 7. _____

Name _____

Exercise!

Do you like to exercise? Exercise is good for you. Walking and running are good ways to exercise. So are swimming and biking. Some people like to do push-ups, sit-ups and jumping jacks. Exercise can help you feel good. It can make your body stronger, too. What is your favorite kind of exercise?

Unscramble.

_____ is good for you.

```
s r E c x i e e
7 4 1 5 2 6 3 8
```

Write.

| walking |
| swimming |
| biking |
| running |

_____

_____

_____

_____

Check.

What do some people do for exercise?

☐ push-ups ☐ sleep ☐ jumping jacks ☐ sit-ups

Circle.

Yes or No

Exercise can help you feel good.	Yes	No
Exercise is very easy.	Yes	No
Exercise can make your body stronger.	Yes	No

• Draw a picture of **you** exercising.

SCIENCE

Name _____

Pyramiding Foods

Read the names of the foods in the Word Bank. Write the words on the lines under the correct food group.

Word Bank: carrots   cherries   chicken   cheese   fish   ham   cake   lettuce   bagel   oranges   pears   rolls   beans   toast   pie   yogurt   candy bar   cottage cheese

dairy

meats

fruits

sweets

vegetables

grains

Name _____

Leaf Shapes

All leaves are not the same. They have different shapes. There are four common shapes.

Draw a line to match the leaf with its shape.

Find some leaves outside.
Try to match them to the shapes.

SCIENCE

Name _____

Tree Parts

Trees have three main parts. They are the trunk, the roots, and the leaves. Each part has a special job. Each part helps the tree.

Cut out the name of each part.
Cut out the job of each part.
Paste them on the picture.
Color the tree.

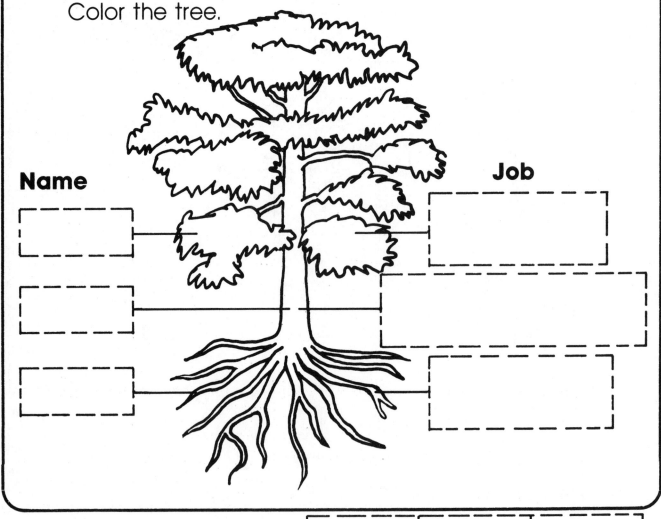

Name

Job

| trunk | leaves | roots |

| I hold the tree in the ground. | I make food for the tree. | I hold most of the tree above the ground. |

Name _____

Leaf Study

Put a leaf under the box on this paper. Rub the paper with the side of your crayon. Use the ruler at the bottom to measure your leaf.

This is a rubbing of my leaf.

1. The color of my leaf is _____ .

2. My leaf is _____ cm wide and _____ cm long.

3. My leaf feels like _____ .

4. I found my leaf _____ .

SCIENCE

Name _____

Food Factories

> Green leaves are like little factories. They make food for the tree. Leaves need sunshine, air, and water to make food.
>
> Leaves change in the fall. They lose their green color. Then they cannot make food for the tree.

Draw a leaf.
This leaf can make food.
Color it green.

Draw another leaf.
This leaf cannot make food.
Color it with pretty fall colors.

Write the correct word.

green yellow
_____

Food is made by _____ leaves.

shade sunshine
_____

Leaves need _____ to make food.

can cannot
_____

Leaves _____ make food in the fall.

Name _____

My Leaf Collection

Attach a leaf and fill in the blanks.

Teacher: Provide each student with three or more copies of this page so booklets can be made.

Tree _____
Location _____
Date _____

SCIENCE

Name _____

From Acorn to Mighty Oak

Some trees drop their seeds in the spring. Other trees drop their seeds in the fall. The seeds grow up. Do you know what they grow up to be?

Show how the acorn grows into a mighty oak tree. Write first, second, or third under the pictures to put them in order. Color the pictures.

Finish the story.

I am a little acorn. One day _____

_____

_____

_____

Plant Parts

A plant has many parts. Each part has a special job.

Word Bank roots   stem
             flower   leaf

Label the parts of the plant.

_____
- - - - - - - - - - - - - - - - -
_____

_____
- - - - - - - - - - - - - - - - -
_____

_____
- - - - - - - - - - - - - - - - -
_____

_____
- - - - - - - - - - - - - - - - -
_____

Draw a line from the plant part to its job.

I make the seeds. ●
I make food for the plant. ●
I take water from the roots to the leaves. ●
I hold the plant in the ground. ●

Color the roots red.
Color the stem yellow.
Color the leaves green.
Color the flower your favorite color.

SCIENCE

Growing Words

Name _____

Write each word on the line below the correct picture.

pumpkin   seed   sprout   flower   plant

_____   _____

- - - - - - - - - - -   - - - - - - - - - - -

_____   _____

_____

- - - - - - - - - - -

_____

_____   _____

- - - - - - - - - - -   - - - - - - - - - - -

_____   _____

Name _____

Edible Plant Parts

We eat many plant parts. Sometimes we eat just the fruit. Sometimes we eat just the leaves. We also might eat the stem, the root, or the seed.

Draw a line from the picture to the name of the plant part.

Color the plant part.

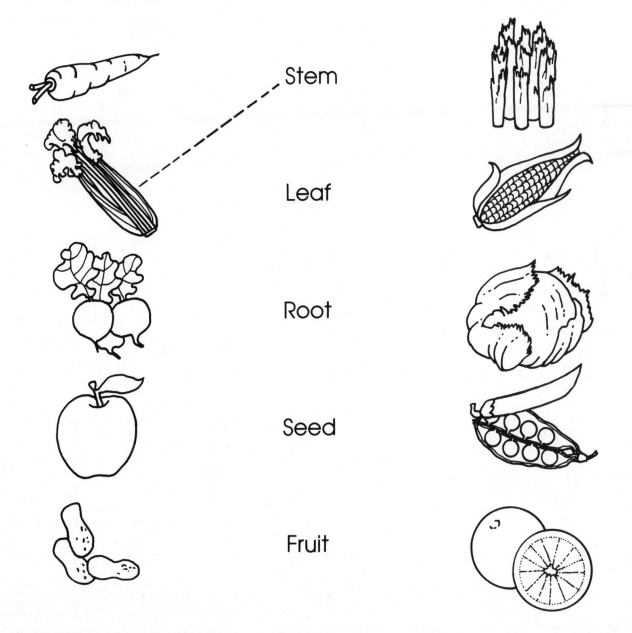

Stem

Leaf

Root

Seed

Fruit

SCIENCE

Name _____

Plant It Right!

Mr. Right and Mr. Wrong planted gardens. Mr. Right planted his garden in the sun. Mr. Wrong planted his garden in the shade. Both of them gave their gardens love and care.

Draw what Mr. Right's garden will look like.

Draw what Mr. Wrong's garden will look like.

Name _____

Water, Please!

Mrs. Right planted her flower seeds last week. She planted them in the sun. She gave her flowers water.

Draw what Mrs. Right's flowers will look like.

Mrs. Wrong planted her flower seeds last week. She planted them in the sun. But she forgot to give them water.

Draw what Mrs. Wrong's flowers will look like.

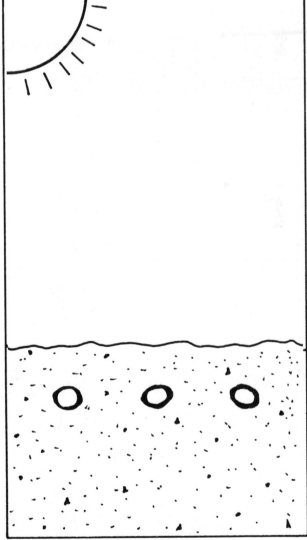

SCIENCE

Daily Learning Drills Grade 1

Name _____

All in the Family

Put an **X** on the animal that does not belong.

1.

2.

3.

4.

5.

Name _____

Animals on the Go

How do these animals move?

Write **walk**, **fly** or **swim**.

_____
- - - - - - - - - -
_____

_____
- - - - - - - - - -
_____

_____
- - - - - - - - - -
_____

Daily Learning Drills Grade 1

SCIENCE

Name _____

Pond Community

Many animals make their homes in a pond community, but some of the animals in this picture do not belong.

Draw an **X** on the animals that do **not** belong.

Name _____

Grassland Community

Many animals make their homes in a grassland community, but some of the animals in this picture do not belong.

Draw an **X** on the animals that do **not** belong.

SCIENCE

Name _____

Ocean Community

Many animals make their homes in an ocean community, but some of the animals in this picture do not belong.

Draw an **X** on the animals that do **not** belong.

Name _____

Forest Community

Many animals make their homes in a forest community, but some of the animals in this picture do not belong.

Draw an **X** on the animals that do **not** belong.

Daily Learning Drills Grade 1

Name _____

Animals at Home

Did you ever see a fish living in a tree? Of course you didn't! Fish live in the water. Help the animals find their homes.

Cut out each animal.
Paste it on its home.
Color the picture.

squirrel   robin   fish   bee

Name _____

Where's My Baby?

Match the adult animal to the baby animal!

sheep

cat

hen

pig

dog

duck

cow

goose

goat

horse

chick

calf

gosling

kitten

piglet

duckling

kid

lamb

puppy

foal

SCIENCE

Name _____

Feathered Friends

Name the parts of the bird.

_____

_____

_____

_____

Read the riddle. Name each bird part.

I keep a bird warm and dry. What am I? _____

I help a bird stand or swim. What am I? _____

I help a bird eat. What am I? _____

I make a bird fly high in the sky. What am I? _____

Word Bank			
feathers	feet	bill	wings

Name _____

My Bird List

Bird watchers keep a list of all the different kinds of birds they have seen. They also keep track of the date and location. Begin a list of your own using the chart below.

Bird	Date	Location

SCIENCE

Name _____

I Slither and Crawl

Do the puzzle about reptiles.
Color only the reptiles.

Across

2. A reptile's skin has _____ .

5. A _____ is a reptile with no legs.

Down

1. A _____ is a reptile with a hard shell on its back.

3. Reptiles are _____ -blooded animals.

4. Baby reptiles hatch from _____ .

Word Bank				
eggs	cold	scales	snake	turtle

Name _____

A Reptile Riddle

Circle the animal that does not belong in the group. Print the letters beside the circled words in the spaces below to find the answer to the riddle.

Birds
1. L   robin
   N   bluebird
   I   cow
   J   crow

Insects
2. L   snake
   A   ladybug
   N   wasp
   T   bee

Dogs
3. B   collie
   I   beagle
   S   shepherd
   L   ox

Reptiles
4. R   snake
   I   horse
   G   turtle
   W   alligator

Farm Animals
5. G   tiger
   K   pig
   O   cow
   Y   hen

Jungle Animals
6. J   lion
   B   cheetah
   U   tiger
   A   rat

Zoo Animals
7. M   bear
   O   giraffe
   T   dog
   F   zebra

Ocean Animals
8. H   octopus
   T   whale
   K   shark
   O   camel

Fish
9. R   raccoon
   I   perch
   V   catfish
   L   tuna

Riddle
What do you call a sick crocodile?

An . . .

$\overline{}_1\ \overline{}_2\ \overline{}_3\ \overline{}_4\ \overline{}_5\ \overline{}_6\ \overline{}_7\ \overline{}_8\ \overline{}_9$

Daily Learning Drills Grade 1

Name _____

I'm Slippery and Cold

Do the puzzle about amphibians.
Color only the amphibians.

Down

1. Amphibian babies usually hatch from _____.
2. Amphibians are _____ -blooded animals.
4. Amphibians often have smooth, moist_____.

Across

3. Amphibian babies breathe with either lungs or
   _____ .

5. Amphibians live in the water and on_____ .

Word Bank				
land	gills	skin	eggs	cold

Name _____

From Mice to Whales

Do the puzzle about mammals.

Color only the mammals.

Down

1. Mammals are _____ -blooded.
4. Mammals breathe with _____ .

Across

2. A mammal's body is usually covered with _____ .
3. Mother mammals feed _____ to their babies.
5. Mammal's _____ are born alive.

Word Bank				
hair	babies	lungs	milk	warm

SCIENCE

Name _____

Just Hanging Around

Bats like to fly at night.
They sleep in the daytime. A
bat sleeps by hanging
upside down. Most bats live
in trees and caves. Have you
ever seen a bat?

night   noon
- - - - - - - - - - - -

Bats like to fly at _____.

Bats sleep in the   room.
                     daytime.

How do bats sleep?

Most bats live in: ☐ trees
                    ☐ caves
                    ☐ floor

the bats black.

• Draw and color a cave with sleeping bats in it.

Name _____

Crawling with Insects

Do the puzzle about insects.

Color only the insects.

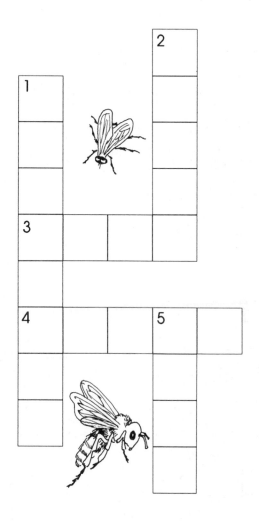

Down

1. Insects have a hard outer _____ .
2. Many insects have two pairs of _____ .
5. Insects have simple and compound _____ .

Across

3. Insects have three pairs of _____ .
4. Insects have _____ main body sections.

Word Bank				
skeleton	legs	wings	three	eyes

SCIENCE

Name _____

Spinning Spiders

There are many kinds of spiders. Spiders have eight legs. They like to eat insects. Many spiders spin a web. The web is the spider's home. Have you ever seen a spider's web?

eight   four
_____

- - - - - - - - - - - - -

Spiders have _____ legs.

I spin a   week.
                 web.

The web is my   kite.
                      home.

What do spiders like to eat?   ☐ insects
                                ☐ jelly

8 black legs on this spider.
3 black spiders on the big web.

• Draw and color a spider and its web.

Name _____

Fish for Me

Do the puzzle about fish.

Color only the fish.

Down

1. Fish have _____ , not legs.
3. A fish's body is often covered with _____ .

Across

2. Fish breathe through _____ .
4. A fish is a _____ -blooded animal.
5. Fish live in the sea and fresh _____ .

Word Bank
water   scales   cold   fins   gills

Daily Learning Drills Grade 1

SCIENCE

Name _____

"Hatch" Something Up

Many animals are hatched from eggs.

Read the clues. Then use the Word Bank to write the name of the correct animal on each egg.

I am a reptile.
I have big, sharp teeth.
I live near a river.

I live most of my life in water.
I eat tadpoles and water insects.
I can pull myself inside my shell.

I have feathers.
I have webbed feet.
I swim in a pond.
I quack with my bill.

I have feathers.
I live on a farm.
I have wings and make peeping
  sounds with my beak.

I live near water.
I eat insects.
I have a tail when I hatch,
  but I lose it as I grow.
I can leap up to six feet.

Word Bank

snake

chick

frog

mud turtle

duck

alligator

Name _____

Butterfly – Part 1

Cut out the butterfly.
Cut out the egg.
Paste them on the milkweed leaf.

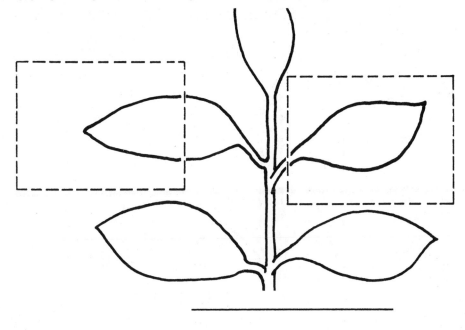

The butterfly lays one _____ on a milkweed

_____
- - - - - - - - - -
_____ .

Word Bank

leaf

egg

Name _____

Butterfly – Part 2

Cut out the caterpillar.
Paste it on the milkweed leaf.
Color the caterpillar black, white, and yellow.

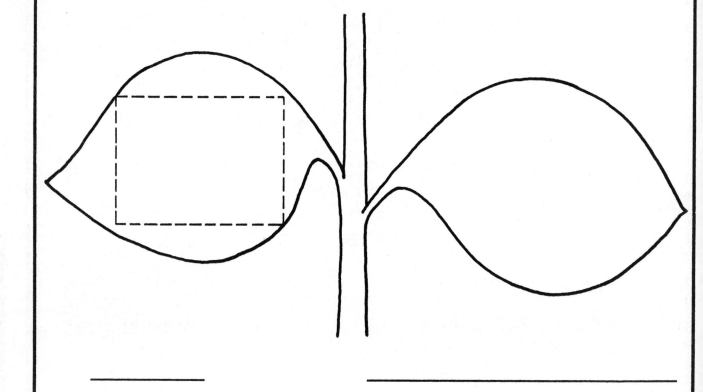

_____   _____

The _____ hatches into a _____.

Word Bank
egg
caterpillar

Name _____

Butterfly – Part 3

Cut out the caterpillar and its food.
Paste them on the milkweed plant.

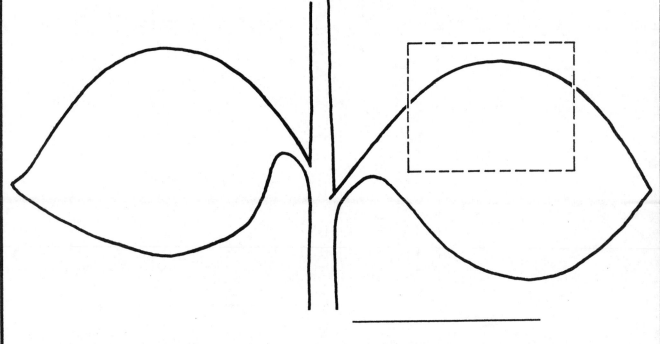

_____

- - - - - - - - - - - - - - -

The hungry caterpillar eats the _____ .

_____

- - - - - - - - - - - - - - -

The caterpillar is _____ .

Word Bank

leaf
growing

Name _____

Butterfly – Part 4

Cut out the chrysalis.
Paste it in place.

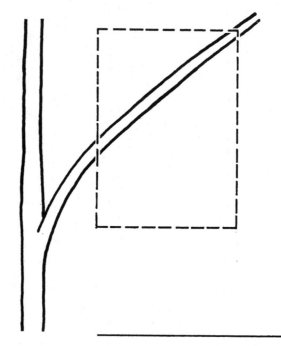

_____

- - - - - - - - - - - - -

The caterpillar is ready to _____ .

_____

- - - - - - - - - - - -

It forms a pale _____ chrysalis.

Word Bank

green
change

Name _____

Butterfly – Part 5

Cut out the butterfly.
Paste it in place.

The _____ is now a butterfly.

The _____ flies away.

Word Bank

butterfly
caterpillar

Name _____

Metamorphosis

Show how the monarch changes.
Cut out the pictures.
Paste them in order.

Word Bank
butterfly

_____
- - - - - - - - - - - - - - - - - - -

The life cycle of a _____
is called metamorphosis.

Name _____

Migration

Cut out the animals.
Paste them in place.

_____
- - - - - - - - - -

It is hard to find _____ in the winter.

_____
- - - - - - - - - -

It is hard to stay _____ in the winter.

Some animals move to warmer places then.
This is called migration.

Word Bank

warm
food

Daily Learning Drills Grade 1

Name _____

Active Animals

Cut out the animals.
Paste them in place.

It is winter.
Deep snow covers the ground.

_____
- - - - - - - - - - - - - - - -

Some animals can find _____ .

_____
- - - - - - - - - - - - - - - -

Some animals can stay _____ .

These animals stay active in winter.

Word Bank
food
warm

Name _____

Storing Food

Cut out the beaver.
Paste him by the hole in the ice.
Trace the path to the beaver's lodge.

Some animals store food for _____ .

The beaver stores food in his _____ .

Word Bank
lodge
winter

SCIENCE

Name _____

Hibernation

Cut out the fat woodchuck.
Paste him by his hole.
Trace the path to the
woodchuck's home.

Some animals hibernate in the winter.

_____

The woodchuck grows a layer of _____ in the fall.

_____

His heartbeat goes _____. His temperature goes

_____   _____

_____. He stays in his home while it is _____.

Word Bank
cold
fat
down
down

Name _____

Animals in Winter

Cut out the animal.
Paste it in its place.
Write the animal's name.

This animal hibernates in the winter.

_____

- - - - - - - - - - - - - - - - - -

_____

This animal migrates in the winter.

_____

- - - - - - - - - - - - - - - - - -

_____

This animal stays active in the winter.

_____

- - - - - - - - - - - - - - - - - -

_____

This animal stores food for the winter.

_____

- - - - - - - - - - - - - - - - - -

_____

Word Bank

rabbit
bird
beaver
woodchuck

Name _____

Animal Homes

Follow the directions below to finish the picture.

1. Draw a fish in the lake.

2. Draw a whale in the ocean.

3. Draw a dog beside the river.

4. Draw a goat on the mountain.

5. Draw a bird on the island.

6. Now color the picture.

Name _____

Blooms and Birds

It is warm in the spring. Flowers begin to bloom. Trees have new . Birds make their nests and lay eggs. Do you like to fly a kite in the spring?

warm   last
_____

It is _____ in the spring.

What can you see in the spring?

What do birds do in the spring?

☐ Birds make nests.

☐ They lay eggs.

☐ They wash dishes.

• Draw and color a nest with four eggs in it.

Name _____

Fun in the Sun

Summer can be very
hot. It is the time when kids
are out of school. They have
fun playing with friends,
swimming to keep cool,
and sometimes going on
family picnics and vacations.

purple   hot
_____
_ _ _ _ _ _ _ _ _ _ _ _ _ _ _
Summer can be very   _____ .

What happens in the summer?

☐ Kids are out of school.

☐ Skunks go on picnics.

☐ Kids play with friends.

What do you like to do in the summer?

_____
_ _
_____
_ _
_____

• Draw and color a picture of your family on vacation.

Name _____

Autumn Leaves

The air gets cool in the autumn. Kids go back to school. Animals store food for the winter. Leaves turn red, yellow and orange. It is a pretty time of the year.

_____time_____cool_____

 The air gets _____ in the autumn.

 What happens in the autumn?

☐ Kids go back to school.

☐ Animals store food.

☐ The air is very hot.

 red   yellow   orange

• Draw and color an autumn tree.

Name _____

Winter Warm-ups

Winter can be cold and snowy. Animals stay near each other to keep warm. People wear coats, hats and . Kids can make a snowman. It is fun to play in the snow.

Winter can be:
- [ ] cold
- [ ] snowy
- [ ] purple

like   warm

We try to stay _____.

What do people wear in the winter?

gloves   hat   pan   coat

a black [hat] on the [snowman].

• Draw and color a snowman.

Name _____

The Four Seasons

1. Cut out and paste the season
   words on the correct boxes below.

2. Color the clothes for:
   Fall – blue; Winter – red;
   Spring – green; Summer – yellow

Spring   Summer

Fall   Winter

SCIENCE

Name _____

Frederick's Furry Friends

Draw picture details of the four seasons around each of Frederick's furry friends. the pictures and each mouse.

Spring Mouse

Summer Mouse

Fall Mouse

Winter Mouse

Name _____

Magnetic Attraction

Draw a line from the magnet to each thing that it can pull.

Name _____

Sticky Hunt

What things will a magnet stick to?

Make lists of the things in your room that will and will not stick to a magnet.

Magnets stick to:	Magnets do not stick to:
_____ ----------------- _____ ----------------- _____ _____ ----------------- _____ _____ ----------------- _____ _____ -----------------	_____ ----------------- _____ ----------------- _____ _____ ----------------- _____ _____ ----------------- _____ _____ -----------------

Caution: Do not try your magnet on these things.

TV	Computer disks
VCR	Cassette tapes
Computer	Video tapes
Radio	Credit cards
Tape recorder	Telephone

Name _____

Opposites Attract

Every magnet has a north pole and a south pole. When you hold two magnets together, this is what happens:

If a north pole and a south pole are next to each other, the magnets attract each other.

If two north poles or two south poles are next to each other, the magnets repel each other.

Tell what each pair of magnets below will do. If the magnets will attract each other, color them red. If the magnets will repel each other, color them blue.

SCIENCE

Name _____

Our Planet Earth

Earth is a planet. It is the planet where we live. Earth has land and water. It gets light and heat from the sun. Earth has one moon. Many people think there is life on other planets. Earth is the only planet that we know has life. Do **you** think there is life on other planets?

Unscramble.

Earth is the _____ where we live.

letpna
256143

Check.

☐ I have land and water.
☐ I get light and heat from the sun.
☐ I have five moons.
☐ I have one moon.
☐ I am a planet.

Circle.

Earth is the only planet that we know has   stars.
life.

Color.

Draw one yellow moon in the picture.

• Draw and color a picture of Earth.

Name _____

Man on the Moon

Do you ever look at the moon at night? The moon travels around the Earth. It gets its light from the sun. Men have gone to the moon in spaceships. They have walked on the moon. They even came back with moon rocks to study. Would you like to walk on the moon?

Circle.
The moon travels around the   room.
                                 Earth.

Write.
The moon gets its light from the _____.
                                 Earth   sun

Check.
How did men go to the moon?   ☐ spaceships
                              ☐ automobiles

Circle.
Yes or No

Men have walked on the moon.   **Yes   No**

Circle.
                                      stars
What did men bring back from the moon?
                                      rocks

Color.
Draw a red spaceship on the moon.

• Draw what you would do if you went to the moon.

SCIENCE

Name _____

A Falling Star

Have you ever seen a falling star? Falling stars are not really stars. They are small pieces of rock. As falling stars fall, they get hot and burn. They look big because they give off so much light. That is why they are so bright in the night sky. Did you know that meteor is another name for a falling star?

Circle.

Yes or No

A falling star is really a star.   Yes   No

Falling stars are pieces of rock.   Yes   No

Falling stars burn as they fall.   Yes   No

Check.

Why does a falling star give off light?

☐ It gets hot and burns.

☐ It has a light bulb in it.

Unscramble.

Another name for a falling star is _____.

e r m o t e
2 6 1 5 3 4

Color.

Draw two yellow falling stars in the picture.

• Write a poem about a falling star.

Name _____

Far Out!

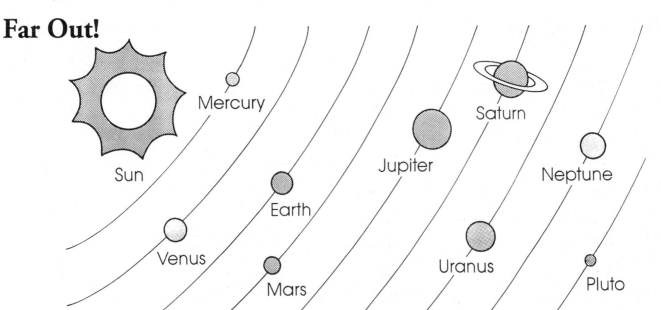

Imagine that you are traveling from the sun to outer space. Write Sun first. Then write the names of the planets in order starting with Mercury.

1. _ _ _ _ _ _ _ _ _ _ _ _ _

2. _ _ _ _ _ _ _ _ _ _ _ _ _

3. _ _ _ _ _ _ _ _ _ _ _ _ _

4. _ _ _ _ _ _ _ _ _ _ _ _ _

5. _ _ _ _ _ _ _ _ _ _ _ _ _

6. _ _ _ _ _ _ _ _ _ _ _ _ _

7. _ _ _ _ _ _ _ _ _ _ _ _ _

8. _ _ _ _ _ _ _ _ _ _ _ _ _

9. _ _ _ _ _ _ _ _ _ _ _ _ _

10. _ _ _ _ _ _ _ _ _ _ _ _

Flip Fun! Draw what you think life could be like on another planet.

Name _____

Twinkling Starlights

Stars change as they get older. They start out big and then shrink. As they shrink, they change color. Color the stars the correct color.

red

orange

yellow

blue

Look at all of these stars. Color each star the correct color. Then draw a circle around the youngest stars and a box around the oldest ones.

Name _____

Me, Myself, and I

1. Tell about yourself on the lines below.

2. Then draw a picture of yourself.

My name is _____ .

The color of my eyes is _____ .

The color of my hair is _____ .

This is me!

SOCIAL STUDIES

Name _____

I Am Special

1. Color the letters in the word [SPECIAL].

2. Cut and paste [SPECIAL] in the [ ] below.

3. Color the objects below.

4. Write a story telling why you are special.

I am [   ]   because:

Name _____

All About Me

Color and write.

My name
_____
- -
_____

My school
_____
- -
_____

My street
_____
- -
_____

My phone
_____
- -
_____

My city
_____
- -
_____

My state
_____
- -
_____

SOCIAL STUDIES

Name _____

Birthday Surprise!

1. Complete sentences 1 and 2.

2. Connect the numbers in the dot-to-dot.

3. Color 2 presents red and 3 presents blue.

4. Draw candles on the dot-to-dot picture to show how old you are.

5. Color the dot-to-dot.

1. My birthdate is _____ ____ ____ .
   month   date   year

2. I am _____ years old.

Name _____

Birthday Bonus Poster

My Cake

_____'s Birthday

_____(date)

How I'll Look

Where I'll Celebrate

Age I'll Be
(Make a big number
and decorate it.)

Friends I'll Invite
(Write their names and
draw their pictures.)

My Gifts

TO:
FROM:

My Birthday Dinner
(Draw what you'd like.)

SOCIAL STUDIES

Name _____

Create a Cinquain — A Poem About Me

Line 1 = 1 word

Line 2 = 2 words describing line 1 (adjectives)

Line 3 = 3 action words (ending in ing)

Line 4 = a phrase expressing a feeling or observation about line 1

Line 5 = a word renaming or describing line 1

School

fun, exciting

learning, studying, playing

a great place to be

Elementary

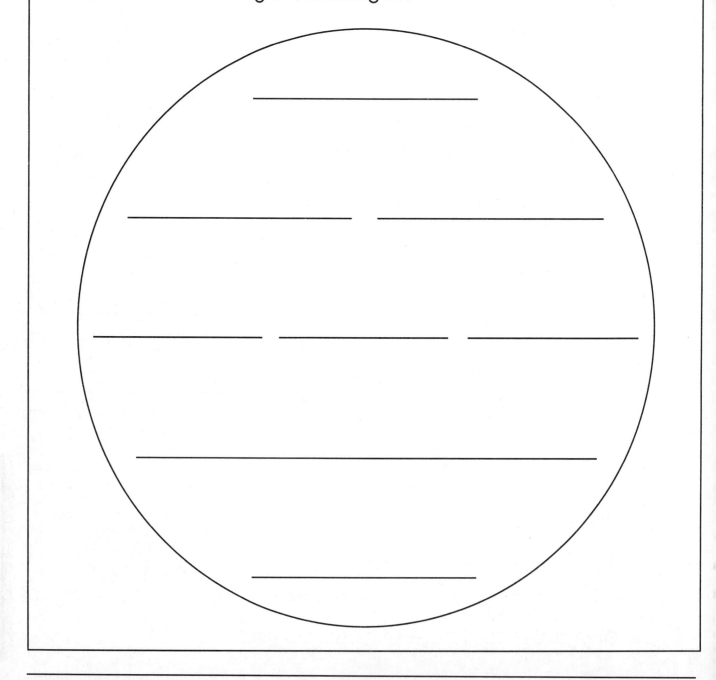

Name _____

Feeling Fantastic!

People can have many feelings. They can be happy. They can be sad. Sometimes people can feel angry. Everyone has feelings.

 People can have many _____ five.

feelings.

happy

angry

sad

 _____

 Make the faces look:

happy   sad   angry

• Draw and color a picture of how you feel.

SOCIAL STUDIES

Name _____

Silly Me

Copy and finish each sentence.

When I feel happy, I...

_____

- -

_____

When I feel sad, I...

_____

- -

_____

When I feel silly, I...

_____

- -

_____

When I feel angry, I...

_____

- -

_____

When I feel scared, I...

_____

- -

_____

When I feel excited, I...

_____

- -

_____

Name _____

My Family

1. Color the roof brown.

2. Color the chimney red.

3. Color the bushes green.

4. Draw a picture of your family inside the house.

5. Write your address at the bottom of the page.

My address is _____

_____

SOCIAL STUDIES

Name _____

Family Puzzle

Draw family members, pets or fun things you do with your family over the entire puzzle. Color. Cut apart and give the whole puzzle to a classmate to put together.

"My Mom"

Name _____

Draw a picture of someone in your family.

Write one sentence to tell why this person is special.

_____

_____

Draw a picture of a gift you would like to give this person.

SOCIAL STUDIES

Name _____

Fun with Friends

A friend is someone you like very much. Friends play together. Friends help each other, too. It is nice to have many friends.

friend   from

– – – – – – – – – – – – – – – – –

A _____ is someone you like.

Yes or **No**

Friends play together.   Yes   No

Friends are cars.   Yes   No

Friends help each other.   Yes   No

Which are friends?

• Draw and color a picture of you and your friends.

Name _____

Dressed and Ready

1. Draw a picture of you and a friend going to school.

2. Dress you and your friend correctly for the weather.

3. Write your school's name on the sign.

Name _____

Special People

Use the code to name the special people below.

A	C	D	E	F	G	H	I	L	M	O	P	R	T
1	2	3	4	5	6	7	8	9	10	11	12	13	14

Box 1:
___ ___ ___ ___ ___ ___
12 11 9   8   2   4

___ ___ ___ ___ ___ ___ ___
11 5   5   8   2   4   13

Box 2:
___ ___ ___ ___ ___ ___
3   11 2   14 11 13

Box 3:
___ ___ ___ ___
5   8   13 4

___ ___ ___ ___ ___ ___ ___
5   8   6   7   14 4   13

Box 4:
___ ___ ___ ___
10 1   8   9

___ ___ ___ ___ ___ ___ ___
2   1   13 13 8   4   13

Name _____

What's My Job?

 the correct word on each line.   a line to match the sentence.

| pilot | farmer | doctor | builder | plumber | teacher |

_____
A _____ helps us learn new things.

_____
A _____ flies planes many places.

_____
A _____ plants and grows crops.

_____
A _____ fixes many leaky pipes.

_____
A _____ builds new buildings.

_____
A _____ helps people get well.

the pictures.

SOCIAL STUDIES

Name _____

My Teacher Helps Me Learn . . .

1. Circle the words from the Word Bank in the puzzle.
2. Then color the circled words green.
3. Last, write your teacher's name on the bottom line.

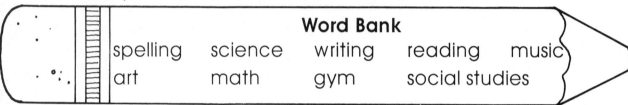

Word Bank

spelling	science	writing	reading	music
art	math	gym	social studies	

r	e	a	d	i	n	g	w	r	i	t	i	n	g
s	o	c	i	a	l	s	t	u	d	i	e	s	x
w	t	y	s	p	e	l	l	i	n	g	b	z	p
o	p	v	s	c	i	e	n	c	e	j	l	x	q
v	w	p	w	m	u	s	i	c	p	q	h	i	r
b	s	c	t	m	a	t	h	w	q	x	z	l	y
t	u	o	a	p	a	r	t	h	o	n	f	k	m
k	m	r	s	z	g	y	m	e	c	d	o	b	n

_____

My teacher's name is _____.

Name _____

Firefighter Find

A firefighter uses many things in his or her job.

Find the words from the Word Bank in the burning house below.

Word Bank			
boots	hat	oxygen mask	gloves
ax	hose	fire engine	ladder

```
o  f  h  p  x  f
x  w  r  n  t  i
y  h  o  s  e  r
g  s  c  l  g  e
e  c  v  a  i  e
n  e  a  d  v  n
m  f  n  d  a  g
a  m  t  e  f  i
s  a  s  r  b  n
k  x  h  a  t  e
b  o  o  t  s  l
g  l  o  v  e  s
```

SOCIAL STUDIES

Name _____

In the Cockpit

A pilot is a person who can fly an airplane. A pilot went to a special school to learn to fly a plane. Some pilots fly planes for fun. Some pilots fly planes as their jobs. A pilot sits in a special part of the plane called the cockpit. Have you ever seen a pilot sitting in the cockpit of a plane?

Write.

The person who flies an airplane is a _____.

point   pilot

Circle.

Yes or No

A pilot went to a special school.	Yes	No
Some pilots fly just for fun.	Yes	No
A pilot drives a school bus.	Yes	No
Some pilots fly planes as their jobs.	Yes	No

Circle.

Where does a pilot sit to fly an airplane?

 cockpit   bench

kitchen

Color.

Put green **X**'s on the pilots.

• Draw a picture of a cockpit with **you** as the pilot.

Name _____

On the Farm

Farmers have a very important job. They grow most of the food that we eat. Some farmers grow plants such as oats, corn and wheat. Some farmers raise animals for food. They sell milk from cows. They sell eggs from chickens. Many farmers use machines to help them do their work.

Circle.

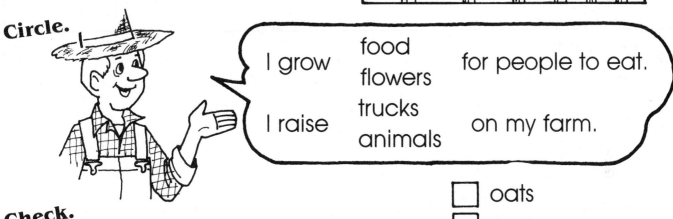

I grow | food / flowers | for people to eat.

I raise | trucks / animals | on my farm.

Check.
What plants do some farmers grow?

☐ oats
☐ corn
☐ steaks
☐ wheat

Match.
Which food comes from which animal?

milk   chickens

eggs   cows

Circle the words in the puzzle above.

• Draw a picture of three farm animals.

SOCIAL STUDIES

Name _____

We Care for You

Doctors help many people. They help sick people get well. They help healthy people stay well. People go to special schools to learn to be doctors. There are many kinds of doctors. There are doctors for children, eye doctors, ear doctors, bone doctors and heart doctors. Would you like to be a doctor?

1→bone

2↓eye

2↓

1→

d
o
c
t
o
r

3→

4 →

3→heart

4→ear

Check.

How does a doctor help people?

☐ A doctor helps sick people get well.

☐ A doctor helps people build houses.

☐ A doctor helps healthy people stay well.

Unscramble.

There are many kinds of _____. Some doctors are

c t o d o s r
3 4 2 1 5 7 6

just for _____.

h d n c l e r i
2 5 8 1 4 7 6 3

Match.

eye doctor
ear doctor
bone doctor
heart doctor

Write.

Fill in the puzzle.

• Write a list of three things you do to stay healthy.

Name _____

Explorers of Space

An astronaut is a person who travels in space. Only a few people can become astronauts. They must be in very good health. They must be very smart. There are special schools to train astronauts. Some astronauts are scientists. Some are pilots. They must work hard to be ready to travel in space.

Unscramble.

A person who travels in space is an _____.

r t n o t s a u a
4 9 6 5 3 2 1 8 7

Check.

☐ Everyone can become an astronaut.

☐ An astronaut must be in very good health.

☐ An astronaut must be very smart.

☐ There are special schools to train astronauts.

Circle.

Some astronauts are: scientists

judges

pilots

Color.

Put a red circle around the **space** words in the picture.

• Draw a picture of where you would like to go in space.

SOCIAL STUDIES

Name _____

When I Grow Up . . .

Draw a line to the correct answer.

1. I want to help sick people.   policeman

2. I want to fly a plane.   teacher

3. I want to help people learn.   artist

4. I want to be in movies.   pilot

5. I want to keep people safe.   doctor

6. I want to help sick animals.   actor

7. I want to paint pretty pictures.   vet

Name _____

I Want to Be . . .

1. Draw a picture of what you might look like when you grow up.

2. Then write what you want to be when you are grown up and why.

When I grow up I want to be a

_____

because . . . _____

_____

_____

_____

_____

_____

_____

_____

Daily Learning Drills Grade 1

SOCIAL STUDIES

Name _____

Making a Map

1. Color and cut out the symbols.

2. Paste the symbols next to the matching words in the map key.

3. Then color the rest of the map.

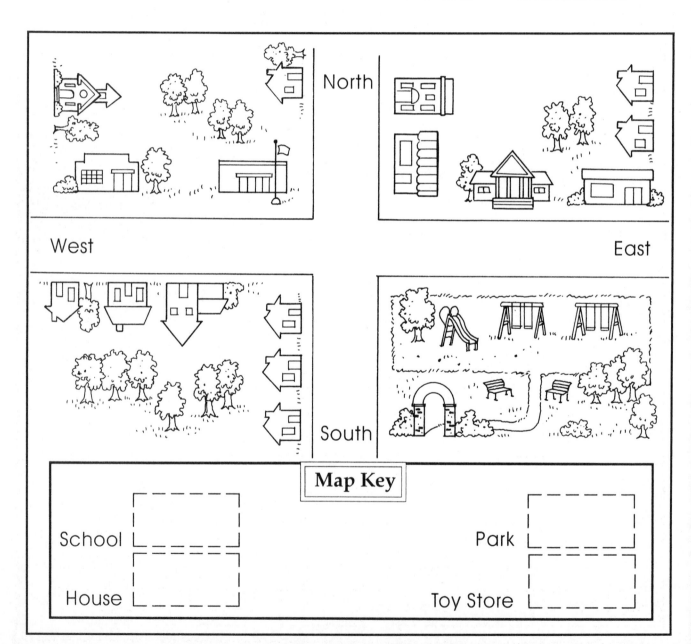

Name _____

A Venice Adventure

1. Start at the gondola, move 2 spaces south. Color the box blue.
2. Go east 2 spaces and draw a brown ⚓ anchor.
3. Go south 2 spaces and put an **X** in that box.
4. Move one space to the west and draw a red △ in that box.
5. Draw an ⚊ oar in the second box south of the △ .
6. Move 2 spaces east to get to the dock at the finish.

Daily Learning Drills Grade 1

SOCIAL STUDIES

Name _____

Class Map

1. Add some symbols of your own to the map key.

2. Make a map of your classroom using the symbols found in the map key.

3. Add N, S, E, and W to your map.

Student's desk

Teacher's desk

_____

_____

Map Key

Name _____

Nick's Neighborhood

Draw a line along the path Nick used to get home.

1. Nick left the library and stopped to play on the school swings.

2. Next he looked at the puppies in the pet store window.

3. Nick watched as the fire truck raced out of the fire station.

4. Then Nick ran home to get money to buy an ice-cream cone.

SOCIAL STUDIES

Name _____

Cities, Towns, and Rural Areas

1. Cut and paste the correct signs on each picture.
2. Draw a door on the barn.
3. Draw another tall building in the city.
4. Color the PARK sign yellow.
5. Write where you live in the last picture.
6. Color the pictures.

Town

Rural Area

City

PARK

I live in a

_____

_____

Name _____

Our State

1. Use a red crayon to outline your state.
2. Color the star yellow and the circle blue.
3. Cut and paste the star where the capital city is located.
4. Cut and paste the circle where your city is located.

5. Complete the sentences below.

This is our state.

The name of our state is _____.

_____ is our capital city.

The city I live in, or near, is _____.

SOCIAL STUDIES

Name _____

Our Country

1. Outline the map green.
2. Color your state blue. Mark an **X** where you live.
3. Color the rest of the map yellow.
4. Trace the sentence at the bottom in black.

This is our country.

Name _____

Scrambled Continents

Unscramble the words below to spell the continents correctly. Remember to cross out the letters you use. Put in capitals where needed. Use the word bank to help you.

1. rtonh miecara __ __ __ __ __   __ __ __ __ __ __

2. cfiara __ __ __ __ __ __

3. eropeu __ __ __ __ __ __

4. uhots ecaamir __ __ __ __ __   __ __ __ __ __ __

5. saia __ __ __ __

6. tnrtaiacac __ __ __ __ __ __ __ __ __ __

7. asurilaat __ __ __ __ __ __ __ __ __

Africa	Australia	North America	Antarctica
	Asia	Europe	South America

SOCIAL STUDIES

Name _____

Land Ho!

1. Draw a ◯ around the word mountains. Then color the mountains black.

2. Draw a ▢ around the word hills. Then color the hills green.

3. Draw a △ around the word plains. Then color the plains brown.

4. Put an **X** under the word water. Then color the water blue.

Name _____

Home Rules

1. Number the pictures in the correct order.
2. Then color the pictures.

Keep your room clean.

Be helpful.

Take care of the yard.

SOCIAL STUDIES

Name _____

School Rules

1. Draw a red circle around the good rules.
2. Draw a black **X** on the bad rules.
3. Then write one of your school rules.

Run in the halls.

Raise your hand in class.

Listen when your teacher talks.

Push friends when standing in line.

Talk anytime in class.

Walk in the halls.

Do not push friends when standing in line.

Fight with friends on the playground.

Be noisy in the library.

Be quiet in the library.

Quietly put school things away.

Stand up when riding the school bus.

Throw paper on the floor.

Clean up your lunch area.

One of our school rules is . . . _____

_____

Name _____

Traffic Signs and Signals

1. Color the STOP sign red.
2. Color the YIELD sign yellow.
3. Do NOT color the DO NOT ENTER sign.
4. Make the TRAFFIC LIGHT green.
5. Color the arrow on the ONE WAY sign black.
6. Color the WALK sign blue.

SOCIAL STUDIES

Name _____

Watch Out!

We should always obey safety rules.

1. Draw a black circle around five things that are wrong in the picture.

2. Then color the picture.

rules

Name _____

Our State's Rules

1. Use the code to complete sentences 1, 2, and 3.

A	C	E	G	I	L	N
1	3	5	7	9	12	14

2. Then write your own answers for sentences 4 and 5.

O	P	R	S	T	V	W
15	16	18	19	20	22	23

1. State rules are called __ __ __ __ .
   12 1 23 19

2. Laws are made in our state __ __ __ __ __ __ __ .
   3 1 16 9 20 1 12

3. The leader of our state is the __ __ __ __ __ __ __ __ .
   7 15 22 5 18 14 15 18

4. We live in the state of _____ .

5. The capital of our state is _____ .

Daily Learning Drills Grade 1

SOCIAL STUDIES

Name _____

Our Nation's Laws

1. Use the Word Bank to write the answers for sentences 1, 2, and 3.

2. Write the name of our nation's President in sentence 4.

3. Draw a picture of our President inside the picture frame.

4. Color the frame and the picture.

Word Bank
President
laws
Washington, D.C.

1. Our nation's rules are called _____ .

2. The White House is in _____ .

3. Washington D.C. is where our _____ lives.

4. Our President's name is _____ .

Name _____

Native American Tribes

1. Color the Indian pictures and the different locations on the map.

2. Cut and paste the pictures correctly on the map.

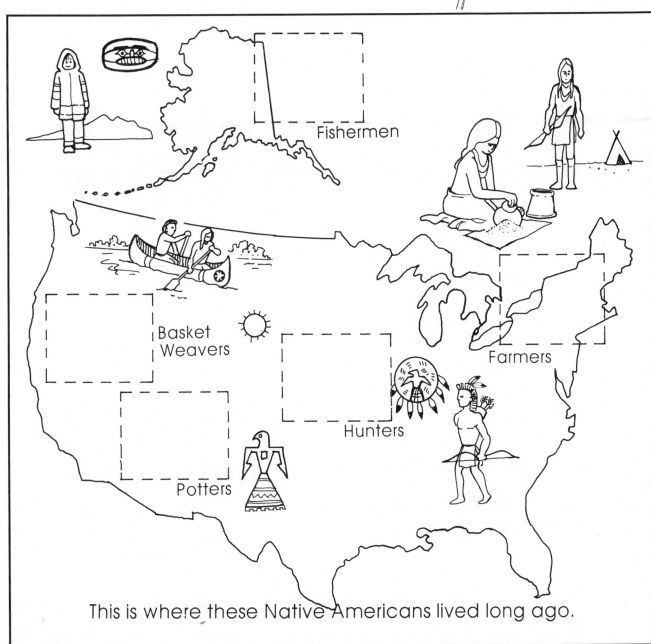

Fishermen

Basket Weavers

Hunters

Farmers

Potters

This is where these Native Americans lived long ago.

SOCIAL STUDIES

Name _____

Native American Homes

1. Write teepee in box 1.

2. Write adobe in box 2.

3. Write wigwam in box 3.

4. Write longhouse in box 4.

5. Draw a sun on the teepee.

6. Color the longhouse brown.

7. Draw a door on the wigwam.

8. Draw small windows on the adobe.

Name _____

Native American Tools

1. Draw a red circle around the corn mortar and the salmon spear.
2. Draw a blue triangle around the digging stick and the fishhook.
3. Draw a green rectangle around the bow and arrow, the canoe paddle, and the hoe.
4. Draw a yellow square around the copper knife and the grinding stones.

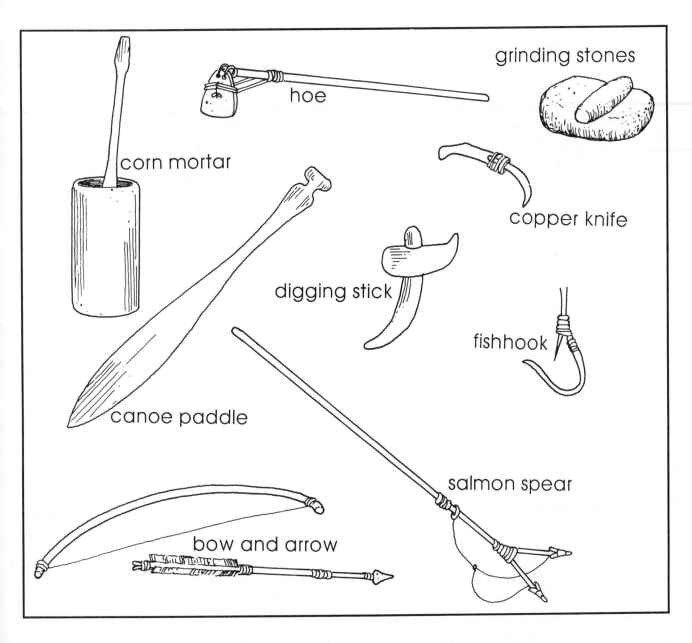

grinding stones

hoe

corn mortar

copper knife

digging stick

fishhook

canoe paddle

salmon spear

bow and arrow

SOCIAL STUDIES

Name _____

The First Thanksgiving

Help the pilgrims find food for their first Thanksgiving.

1. Draw a brown circle around each type
   of food from the Word Bank hidden in
   the picture below.

2. Then color the picture.

Word Bank	
corn	pumpkin
squash	turkey
onion	beans
berries	fish

Name _____

A Whole New World

Write each word on the line next to the matching picture.

| **Word Bank** | berries | corn | plant | Indian | ocean |
| | Pilgrim | ship | quail | forest | turkey |

Daily Learning Drills Grade 1

Name _____

Colonial Workers

1. Draw 👞 shoes in the window for the shoemaker.

2. Make some ☁ dough for the baker to use to make bread.

3. Put a ⚒ hammer in the blacksmith's hand.

4. Draw a 👗 dress on the hanger for the dressmaker.

5. Draw a 〰 saddle for the saddlemaker.

6. Make sacks of 🪹 flour and ☐ sugar for the storekeeper.

Name _____

George Washington

1. Connect the dots beginning with number 1.

2. Color the dot-to-dot.

3. On the lines below write:

   George Washington was our first President.

Name _____

Abraham Lincoln

1. Write the words from the Word Bank under the correct pictures.

2. Then color the pictures.

Word Bank

log cabin
string tie
top hat
White House
ax
books

Abraham Lincoln as a boy | Abraham Lincoln as President

Name _____

Clara Barton

1. Color the  medicine bottle brown.

2. Draw a bandage on the man's leg.

3. Color the cross on the wagon red.

4. Color Clara Barton's bag black.

5. Now color the rest of the picture.

SOCIAL STUDIES

Name _____

Martin Luther King, Jr.

1. Color the W's black.

2. Color the X's blue.

3. Color the Y's brown

4. Color the Z's pink.

5. Color the V's green.

Name _____

Sally Ride

1. Color only the things Sally Ride would need in space.

2. Cut out and paste the colored pictures in the boxes below.

3. Then color Sally Ride.

First Woman in Space – June 1983

SOCIAL STUDIES

Name _____

Person I Most Admire

1. Think about the person you most admire.

2. Complete the sentences below.

3. Then draw a picture of yourself with that person.

The person I most admire is _____ .

I admire this person because _____

_____ .

Name _____

An African Aunt

1. Read each sentence and write the letter on the ant.

2. Then write each letter in order to find the answer to the riddle at the bottom.

1. Find the ninth letter in crocodile.

2. Write the first letter in lion.

3. What is the last letter in giraffe?

4. Find the middle letter in ape.

5. What letter is at the end of cheetah?

6. Write the fifth letter in zebra.

7. Find the last letter in python.

8. Write the third letter in ostrich.

What animal has the biggest aunt?

An __ __ __ __ __ __ __ __ __

SOCIAL STUDIES

Name _____

Chinese Challenge

Use the Word Bank to write the correct words in the sentences.

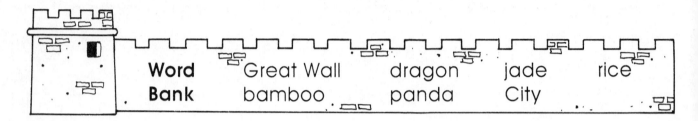

Word   Great Wall   dragon   jade   rice
Bank   bamboo   panda   City

1. It grows in China and rhymes with "can do."

　__ __ __ __ __ __
　1

2. Many Chinese stories are written about this monster.

　__ __ __ __ __ __
　　　7

3. A beautiful green stone. __ __ __ __
　　　　　　　　　　　4

4. This animal could once be found only in China.

　__ __ __ __ __
　　　6

5. Chinese Emperors once lived in the Forbidden __ __ __ __.
　　　　　　　　　　　　　　　　　　3

6. The long wall in China is called the

　__ __ __ __ __ __ __ __ __.
　　2

7. A very important food in the Chinese diet is __ __ __ __.
　　　　　　　　　　　　　　　　　5

Write the numbered letters in order to find the name of this important city in China.

　__ __ __ __ __ __ __
　1 　2 　3 　4 　5 　6 　7

Answer Key

The Alphabet

___ a line to connect the dots. Follow the letters of the alphabet.

Page 1

Under-Cover Work

Color the pictures. Then cut them out and glue onto Ira's sleeping bag in ABC order.

1. bear
2. dinner
3. flashlight
4. pillow
5. Reggie
6. suitcase

Page 2

The Quail Trail

Read the words. Cut and paste them on the quails in alphabetical order.

America courage gathered
joy kind quail
ready thanksgiving wonderful

Page 3

Squeeze a Summer Sipper

Read the words on the juicer. Write them in alphabetical order.

Word Bank
school   apples   leaves
working   playing   blossoms
town   clothes   mowing

1. apples
2. blossoms
3. clothes
4. leaves
5. mowing
6. playing
7. school
8. town
9. working

Page 4

Morris Learns the Alphabet

To help Morris find his way to the candy store write the words from the Word Bank in ABC order.

Word Bank
desk   time
bedtime   climb
moose   yelled
spell   hid
numbers   another

1. another
2. bedtime
3. climb
4. desk
5. hid
6. moose
7. numbers
8. spell
9. time
10. yelled

Page 5

Ghosts and Spaceships

Write the words in ABC order on the correct picture.

Color space word boxes red and blue.
Color Halloween word boxes orange and black.

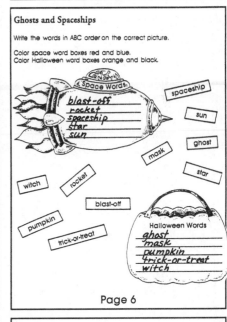

Space Words
blast-off
rocket
spaceship
star
sun

spaceship   sun   ghost   star   mask   rocket   witch   blast-off   pumpkin   trick-or-treat

Halloween Words
ghost
mask
pumpkin
trick-or-treat
witch

Page 6

Alpha-bear-tical Antics

Follow the directions to answer the riddle below. In each paw, print the letter that comes . . .

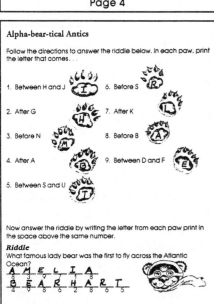

1. Between H and J   I
2. After G   H
3. Before N   M
4. After A   B
5. Between S and U   T
6. Before S   R
7. After K   L
8. Before B   A
9. Between D and F   E

Now answer the riddle by writing the letter from each paw print in the space above the same number.

Riddle
What famous lady bear was the first to fly across the Atlantic Ocean?

A M E L I A
4 6 8 5 2 1

G E A R H A R T
9 7 1 3 4 8 5

Page 7

Letter Lift

Cut out the letter squares. Paste each square on the correct balloon.

a   e   i
o   u   o
Vowels

r   s   m   n
v   g   t   j
x   p   q   h   d
c   k   l   b   f
Consonants

Page 8

"Feast" Your Eyes on This!

Look at the picture. Find and circle the letters that are hidden in the picture that spell **Happy Thanksgiving**. Color the picture.

Page 9

Daily Learning Drills Grade 1

Sea Search

Help the boat sail to the island! Color the fish:
capital letters—orange   **lower-case letters**—blue

Page 10

Take One or Two

Look at each picture on the cookies and read the word below it. Cut and paste each cookie on the correct jar to show how many syllables are in the word.

1 Syllable
card   cut   mop   heart   hug

2 Syllables
mailbox   bathtub   stinkweed   sparkles   paintbrush

Page 11

Two for the Dragon

Cut out the muffins. Glue the six muffins with two-syllable words on the dragon's tummy. Glue the rest in the center of another sheet of drawing paper. Then create and color your own dragon around these muffins.

muffin   dragon   firewood   drawbridge   kingdom   muncher

Bonus
Fill these muffins with your own two-syllable words.

Words will vary

Page 12

Half a Zoo

McGrew needs your help to capture the other half of these new zoo animals. Draw a matching half for each picture on this page and on the next. Color.

Elephant-Cat   Obsk

Tick-Tack-Toe   Iota

Page 13

Warm and Cozy

Look at the picture very carefully. All of the animals are snuggled in different places. Circle the eight animals hidden in the picture. Then color the picture.

rabbit   baager   duck   mouse
mole   hedgehog   fox   squirrel

Page 14

Hidden Pebble Search

Sylvester hid 20 magic pebbles in this picture. Find the pebbles. Color them red and circle them with black. Then color the rest of the picture.

Page 15

Snowy Day

Circle the mistakes in this crazy, snowy-day picture. Then color all parts of the picture.

Page 16

Select a Synonym

Read the words. ___ the word that means almost the same as the first word.

1. big		cold	loud	(large)
2. yell		(shout)	eat	jump
3. small		good	thin	(little)
4. smile		tall	(grin)	soft
5. boat		talk	(ship)	hop
6. look		(see)	fall	laugh

Page 17

Similar Meanings

Read the words in the word box. ___ two words under each picture.

| rock | start | road | begin | street | stone |
| shut | sad | talk | unhappy | speak | closed |

start   rock
begin   stone

road   sad
street   unhappy

talk   shut
speak   closed

Page 18

A Change in the Weather

Change Alexander's cloudy day into a sunny day! Cut and paste an opposite in the ☼ for each ☁ word.

Page 19

Attach an Antonym

Read the word on each person. Find the word above the hair that means the opposite and paste it on that head.

Page 20

In or Out?

Read the words. Find a word in the Word Bank that means the opposite of each word given. Then write it on the line.

1. up — *down*
2. in — *out*
3. sad — *happy*
4. stop — *go*
5. big — *little*
6. on — *off*
7. left — *right*
8. here — *there*
9. yes — *no*
10. mother — *father*

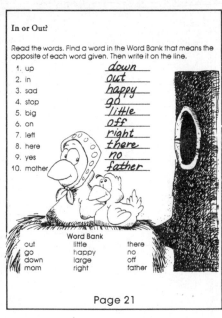

Word Bank

out	little	there
go	happy	no
down	large	off
mom	right	father

Page 21

Same or Opposite?

Color the spaces yellow that have word pairs with opposite meanings. Color the spaces blue that have word pairs with the same meanings.

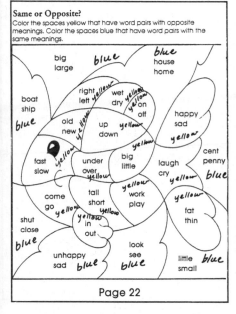

Page 22

Two Words in One

✏ the two words that make up each compound word below.

snowball — *snow* / *ball*
raincoat — *rain* / *coat*
airplane — *air* / *plane*
watermelon — *water* / *melon*
haircut — *hair* / *cut*
football — *foot* / *ball*
fingernail — *finger* / *nail*
sunshine — *sun* / *shine*

Page 23

It's Raining Meatballs!

Draw a line from each word in List A to a word in List B to make a compound word. On another piece of paper, write the compound words and draw pictures of them.

List A

List B

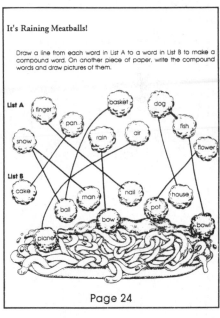

Page 24

"Compound"-ing the Cave's Echo

Read the words in the Word Bank. Find the two words that go together to make a compound word and write it on a bat.

bath	bed	bee
birth	by	comb
cow	day	every
fire	flies	for
got	grass	hide
hive	honey	lands
lights	near	room
one		street
spread		

bathroom
birthday
fireflies
beehive
cowhide
forgot
streetlights
everyone
nearby
bedspread
honeycomb
grasslands

Page 25

Let's Make a Snowman

✏ a line from each pair of words to the right contraction.

he is — it's
it is — she's
she is — he's
they are — you're
you are — they're
we are — i'm
I am — we're

Page 26

Loppy Ears

A contraction is a short way to write two words. Choose a contraction from the big carrot and print it on the lines.

1. Leo *can't* get his ears to stand up tall.
2. *It's* not fun to be teased by the others.
3. "*I'm* not normal," thought Leo.
4. Doing ear exercises *didn't* help Leo.
5. *I'll* go see the possum, he'll know what to do.
6. *He's* my good friend.
7. The other bunnies *couldn't* get their ears to flop down.
8. *We're* all normal because we are loved.

I'm We're couldn't can't He's didn't
I'll It's

Page 27

Daily Learning Drills Grade 1

"Crumb"-y Contractions

Read the two words on the bread crumbs. Find the contraction in the Word Bank and write it on the bird.

we're — we / are
that's — that / is
I'd — would
I'll — I / will
she's — she / is
they're — they / are
she'd — she / would
let's — let / us
we'd — we / would

Word Bank:
we'd   she's
let's   I'll
I'd   we're
they're
that's
she'd

Page 28

Barnyard Nouns

A noun is a naming word.
A noun names a person, place or thing.

Find two nouns in each sentence below. ___ them.

1. The pig has a curly tail.
2. The hen is sitting on her nest.
3. A horse is in the barn.
4. The goat has horns.
5. The cow has a calf.
6. The farmer is painting the fence.

Page 29

Nouns on the Farm

tree, sun, barn, ducks, horse, pig, girl, boy, farmer

Read the naming words below. ___ the correct naming word for each picture of a person, place or thing.

barn   farmer   pig
boy   tree   horse
girl   ducks   sun

Page 30

Action Match

Find the action word in each sentence. ___ it.
___ a line to match each sentence with the correct picture.

1. The dog barks.
2. The bird flies.
3. A fish swims.
4. One monkey swings.
5. A turtle crawls.
6. A boy talks.

Page 31

Circus Action

A verb is an action word. A verb tells what a person or thing does or did.

Find the verb in each sentence below and ___ it.

1. The bear climbs a ladder.
2. Two tiny dogs dance.
3. A boy eats cotton candy.
4. A woman swings on a trapeze.
5. The clown falls down.
6. A tiger jumps through a ring.

Page 32

Falling Verbs

___ only the leaves that have verbs.

read, rabbit, baby, hops, father, dig, fish, looked, truck, city, jumps, walked, claps, drank

Page 33

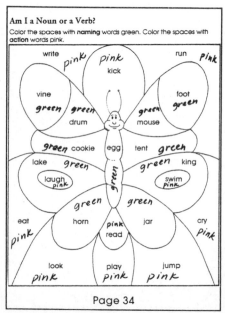

Am I a Noun or a Verb?

Color the spaces with **naming** words green. Color the spaces with **action** words pink.

write — pink
pink — pink
run — pink
kick
vine
green — green
foot
green
drum
mouse
green — cookie
egg
tent — green
lake — green
green — king
laugh — pink
swim — pink
green
green
eat — pink
horn
pink — read
jar
cry — pink
look — pink
play — pink
jump — pink

Page 34

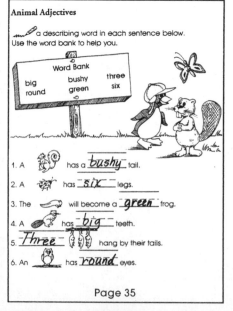

Animal Adjectives

___ a describing word in each sentence below.
Use the word bank to help you.

Word Bank
big   bushy   three
round   green   six

1. A ___ has a _bushy_ tail.
2. A ___ has _six_ legs.
3. The ___ will become a _green_ frog.
4. A ___ has _big_ teeth.
5. _Three_ ___ hang by their tails.
6. An ___ has _round_ eyes.

Page 35

Fishing for Adjectives

___ only the fish with describing words.

rug, funny, loud, bed, warm, pink, green, sad, moan, quilt

Page 36

Daily Learning Drills Grade 1

Corn Crackles

Here are some describing words:

sour furry sweet tasty crisp
tall crunchy cloudy sad soft

Which four words do you think might best describe the cereal? ✎ them on the lines on the cereal box.

crunchy
sweet
tasty
crisp

Page 37

The Turtles Tell

> Some sentences tell something.
> Telling sentences begin with a capital letter.
> Telling sentences end with a period.

✎ only the sentences that tell.

1. Two turtles sat on a log.
2. One turtle fell off.
3. Did you see him?
4. He swam away.
5. The water is cold.
6. Can you swim?

Page 38

All About Dinosaurs

✎ the telling sentences below. Begin each sentence with a capital letter and end with a period.

1. dinosaurs lived long ago

Dinosaurs lived long ago.

2. many were very big

Many were very big.

3. some dinosaurs ate plants

Some dinosaurs ate plants.

4. all the dinosaurs died out

All the dinosaurs died out.

5. no one is sure why

No one is sure why.

Page 39

State It!

> Some sentences tell something. They are called statements. A statement begins with a capital letter and ends with a period.

✎ these statements correctly.

1. jenny planted a seed

Jenny planted a seed.

2. she gave it water

She gave it water.

3. it sat in the sunshine

It sat in the sunshine.

4. the plant began to grow

The plant began to grow.

5. leaves grew large

Leaves grew large.

6. a flower opened

A flower opened.

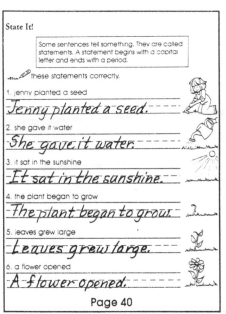

Page 40

Fishy Questions

✎ the first word of each question below. Remember to begin with a capital letter. End each question with a question mark.

1. Is (is) that your boat?
2. Did (did) you catch that fish?
3. How (how) much does it weigh?
4. Will (will) you eat it?
5. Did (did) you fish with worms?
6. Is (is) the water cold?

Page 41

Did You Ask Me Something?

> Some sentences ask something. They are called questions. A question begins with a capital letter and ends with a question mark.

✎ only the questions.

1. Is that your house?
2. There are two pictures on the wall.
3. Where do you sleep?
4. Do you watch TV in that room?
5. Which coat is yours?
6. The kitten is asleep.

Page 42

Period or Question Mark?

Put a period or a question mark at the end of each sentence.

1. Can the fish jump out of the tank ?
2. Two snakes are in that cage .
3. How much does that turtle cost ?
4. Yes, I already have a dog .
5. His name is King .
6. Do you have a dog ?

Page 43

What a Trick!

If the word names an animal, color the space brown.
If the word names something to eat, color the space blue.
If the word names something found in the sky, color the space yellow.
If the word names a piece of furniture, color the space red.
If the word names something you use in school, color the space green.

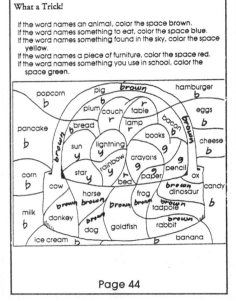

Page 44

Pick a Pouch

Cut and paste each word on the correct kangaroo pouch. Then color one kangaroo green and the other your favorite color.

Animal Words: cat, dog, bear, fish
Color Words: purple, red, blue, green

Page 45

Daily Learning Drills Grade 1

"Cap" the Words

Read the headings on the caps. Write the words from the Word Bank on the correct cap.

How Clothes Can Feel

warm
itchy
stiff
hot

Words That Tell Where

under
over
in
on

Which word is left over? __jacket__

Word Bank

under   over   hot
warm   itchy   in
jacket   stiff   on

Page 46

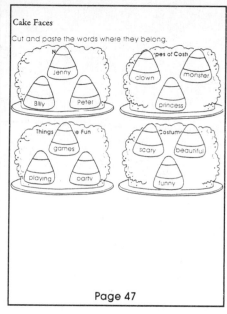

Cake Faces

Cut and paste the words where they belong.

Jenny
clown   monster
Billy   Peter   princess

Things ...e Fun
games
playing   party

...pes of Cost...
scary   beautiful
funny

Page 47

Missing Pieces

Write the puzzle words on the correct lines. Color the pieces as shown

Answers may vary.

People   purple
Betsy   nurse
mayor   man
doctor

Things in a Hospital   red
mask   x-rays
wheelchair   pills
beds

Food   yellow
cake   ham
eggs   bananas
ice cream

Places   green
school   house
hospital   playroom
library

Toys   blue
puzzle   doll
puppet   truck
ball

Page 48

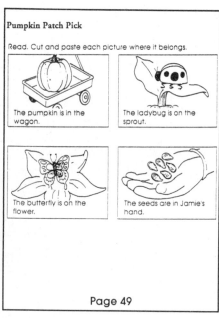

Pumpkin Patch Pick

Read. Cut and paste each picture where it belongs.

The pumpkin is in the wagon.

The ladybug is on the sprout.

The butterfly is on the flower.

The seeds are in Jamie's hand.

Page 49

Down on the Farm

A farm is a home for some animals. Horses, cows and pigs live on a farm. Sheep and chickens are farm animals, too. Many farm animals live in a big barn.

Which animals live on a farm?

ride   farm

A __farm__ is a home for some animals.

Many farm animals live in a big _____.

barn.

• Draw and color two farm animals.

Page 50

My Pet

It is fun to have a pet. Dogs and cats are good pets. Birds and rabbits can be pets, too. Pets are good friends. They need care and love every day.

friends   fast

Pets are good __friends__

long   love

Pets need care and _____.

dog   rabbit   cat   bird

__dog__   __bird__
__cat__   __rabbit__

• Draw and color a picture of your pet.

Page 51

Mixed-up Colors

Did you know that all colors come from red, yellow or blue? They're the primary colors. Red and blue make purple. Blue and yellow make green. Yellow and red make orange. It is fun to mix paint to make new colors.

r and y make o
1   2   4

b and r make p
3   1   5

y and b make g
2   3   6

Circle.
Which three colors do you need to make all colors?
(red)   green   (yellow)   (blue)   pink

Write.
Red, yellow and blue are __primary__ colors.
orange   primary

Match.
Red and blue make ——— orange.
Blue and yellow make ——— purple.
Yellow and red make ——— green.

Color the picture: 1 - red   2 - yellow   3 - blue
4 - orange   5 - purple   6 - green

• Draw and color a picture using the primary colors.

Page 52

Scrambled Shoes

Minnie needs new shoes. She tries on several pairs and decides on one pair. Oops! While trying on all of the shoes, she has scattered them all over. Now she can't find the other shoe of the pair she wants.

Help Minnie find her shoe. Using a different color for each pair of shoes, color each pair exactly the same. Then draw a circle around Minnie's missing shoe.

Page 53

Barbecue Mishap

Meg and her family are barbecuing hamburgers. A gust of wind blows the flames toward a tree. Oh no! The tree is on fire! A fire truck races to the fire.

Trace the different ways the firefighters can get to Meg's house.

How many different ways did you find? __5__

Use a red crayon to trace the quickest way to Meg's house.

Page 54

Musician's Choice

Many different instruments are used to make music. Irene knows how to play several musical instruments.

Irene knows how to play these instruments.

Irene does not know how to play these instruments.

Draw a circle around the instruments Irene probably also knows how to play.

Page 55

Family Portraits

Families may be big or small. No matter how many people are in a family, each person is important to the others.

Cut out the pictures at the bottom of the page. Read the clues. Paste the pictures of the members of this family in the frame where they belong.

- Grandfather is in the middle.
- The girl is on the right end.
- The boy is on the left end.
- Mother is between Grandmother and the boy.
- Father is beside the girl.
- The family dog is between Grandfather and Father.

Page 56

Where Is That Sheep?

Read. Cut and paste each sheep where it belongs. Color the pictures.

The sheep is on the table.

The sheep is under the loom.

The sheep is in the pokeweed berry bush.

The sheep is beside the cloth.

The sheep is on Charlie's hat.

The sheep is in between the pieces of Charlie's cloak.

Page 57

Umbrellas Up!

Look at the pictures. Circle the correct word and write it on the line.

Molly puts ___up___ the umbrella.
(up) on in

The tie is ___on___ the bed.
up (on) in

The cat is ___in___ the house.
up on (in)

The bird flies ___up.___
up on in

He puts ___on___ mittens.
up (on) in

The dog is ___in___ the rain.
up on (in)

Page 58

Playing Parts

Look at each picture. Find the title of the story that Grace is acting out in the Word Bank. Write it under the correct picture.

Space Adventures

Cowboy Jake & the Roundup

The Lost Treasure Chest

The Case of the Missing Cat

Word Bank

The Case of the Missing Cat   Cowboy Jake & the Roundup
Space Adventures   The Lost Treasure Chest

Page 59

It's Time to . . .

Read and write four sentences under the correct pictures.

Susie's alarm clock rings.

Susie picks up her books.

It's time to get up.

It's time to go to school.

Susie is getting hungry.

Susie hears the school bell ring.

It's time to eat lunch.

It's time to go home from school.

Page 60

What Will They Do?

Read each sentence and question. Put a ✓ in the box by the correct answer. Draw a picture to answer the question.

The boy is putting on his skates.
What will he do?
☐ He will go swimming.
✓ He will go skating.

The girl fills her glass with milk.
What will she do?
✓ She will drink the milk.
☐ She will drop the milk.

The lady wrote a letter to her friend.
What will she do?
☐ She will throw the letter away.
✓ She will mail the letter.

The kids gave Sally a birthday gift.
What will she do?
✓ She will open the gift.
☐ She will not open the gift.

Page 61

What Does That Mean?

Read. Color the picture that shows what each sentence really means.

We are just horsing around.

She had a puzzled look.

Pipe down, please.

He is down in the dumps.

The window flew open.

Page 62

Save Six

Color six animals.

Any six.

Color six things that will grow.

Draw pictures of six of your favorite things on the back of this paper.

Page 63

Daily Learning Drills Grade 1

Where's the Hair?

Draw different kinds of hair on each head. Color.

Pictures will vary.

Page 64

Suited for Winter

Read and do.

1. Draw a hat on the snowman. Color the hat **purple** and **orange**.
2. Draw a snowsuit on the snowman. Color the snowsuit **blue**.
3. Draw boots on the snowman. Color the boots **yellow**.
4. Draw mittens on the snowman. Color the mittens **green**.

Page 65

Meet the Alien

1. Color the hands and arms yellow.
2. Print your name on the biggest ▭.
3. Draw a red ⌣ on the face.
4. Put green dots on the ⌒.
5. Color the ▱ purple.
6. Color all of the △'s orange.
7. Draw red and blue stripes on the legs ○.
8. Color the ▢ blue.

Page 66

What's the Idea?

Read the sentence in each speech bubble. Underline the main idea.

My tummy hurts.

The mouse wants more to eat.
The mouse ate too much cheese.

My hat is blowing away.

It is a very windy day.
He doesn't want a hat.

I am seven years old today.

The cake is very big.
Today is her birthday.

I can't find my home.

The cat is lost.
The cat has a new home.

May I have more ice cream?

She likes cake best.
She likes ice cream a lot.

Page 67

Yes or No?

Read each sentence. Circle **yes** if the sentence tells about the picture. Circle **no** if it does not.

The running shoe is very old.
The tree has lost its leaves.
The soup smells good.
Two butterflies sit on flowers.
The dog eats a new bone.
The boy sees the plane.
The snake is lying on a rock.
The spider is spinning its web.

Page 68

Picture Pick

Look at each picture. Read the sentences. ✎ the correct letter in each ○ to tell the main idea.

A - The eggs are ready to hatch.
B - It is a very windy day.
C - The old house is very spooky.
D - The popcorn popper is too full.
E - The girl thinks the music is too loud.
F - It is too warm for a snowman.

✎ the pictures:
A — yellow
B — red
C — blue
D — green
E — orange
F — purple

Page 69

What About Bear?

Read each sentence. Circle **yes** if the sentence tells about the picture. Circle **no** if it does not.

It is a very hot day.
The hat is too small.
The bear is afraid of the mouse.
The bear washed three shirts.
The circus is lots of fun.
The bear has two mittens.
The bear walks to school.
The bear likes to cook.

Page 70

What Did Morris Do Now?

Look at the pictures. Find the sentence in the Word Bank that matches each picture. Write it on the line.

Morris hid his gumdrops.

Morris pretended to be a closet.

Morris was too big for the desk.

Word Bank

Morris hid his gumdrops.
Morris was too big for the desk.
Morris wanted to go home.
Morris was too little for the desk.
Morris pretended to be a closet.

Page 71

What a Life!

Read each sentence. If it tells something that could really happen, paste it under the real dog. If it tells something that is make-believe, paste it under the make-believe dog.

A dog can sit beneath a tree.	A dog can fly a kite.
A dog can splash in the water.	A dog can row a boat.
A dog can walk on a sidewalk.	A dog can be a lead singer.
A dog likes to eat bones.	A dog puts jam on toast.

Page 72

My Friend the Bear

Read each sentence. If it tells something that could really happen, color the real bear. If it tells something that is make-believe, color the toy bear.

	Real	Make-Believe
1. A bear can live in a forest.	✓	
2. A bear can search in a store for a lost button.		✓
3. A girl can sew a button on a pair of overalls.	✓	
4. A bear can talk to a little girl		✓
5. A toy bear can ride up an escalator by himself.		✓
6. A toy bear can sit on a toy department shelf.	✓	
7. A little girl can save money in a piggy bank.	✓	
8. A toy bear and a little girl can be friends.	✓ or	✓
9. A toy bear can yank a button off a mattress.		✓

Page 73

Go for the Snow

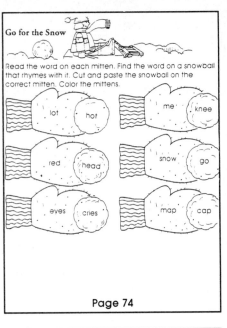

Read the word on each mitten. Find the word on a snowball that rhymes with it. Cut and paste the snowball on the correct mitten. Color the mittens.

lot — hot   me — knee

red — head   snow — go

eyes — cries   map — cap

Page 74

Strawberry Patch Match

Read the word on each strawberry. Find the word in the Word Bank that rhymes. Write it on the line.

sun	*fan*	Sam	*jam*
sky	*high*	day	*away*
bark	*park*	goat	*boat*
kite	*might*	tea	*tree*
flowers	*showers*	cool	*school*

Word Bank

away	boat	high	fun
might	park	tree	jam
showers	school		

Page 75

A Space Case!

Read the word on each spaceship. Find the words in the Word Bank that rhyme and write them on the line.

two — *boo*   small — *tall*   most — *ghost*

rock — *knock*   spotted — *dotted*   door — *four*

cat — *fat*   me — *three*   funny — *bunny*

brown — *clown*

Word Bank

fat	ghost	patch
tall	knock	clown
boo	three	dotted
step	four	bunny

Page 76

Carrot Crop

the four pictures. and the pictures in 1, 2, 3, 4 order.

Page 77

Fall Pick Up

Color the pictures. Cut and paste each picture in 1, 2, 3, 4 order.

Page 78

It's Hard to Wait!

Write 1, 2, 3, or 4 in the boot next to the picture to show the order it happened in the story. Then draw a line from the boot to the sentence that tells about that picture.

1 — He has a new snowsuit.

4 — He made a snowball.

2 — He put on his new snowsuit, boots, hat and mittens.

3 — He wished and wished for snow.

Page 79

How Many?

Read the words in the Word Bank. If the word means one, write it under Buster. If the word means more than one, write it under Sue Ellen.

one
1. *straw*
2. *child*
3. *person*
4. *class*
5. *recess*
6. *tooth*

more than one
1. *teeth*
2. *babies*
3. *men*
4. *children*
5. *people*
6. *patients*

Word Bank

teeth	child	class	people
straw	men	children	tooth
babies	person	recess	patients

Page 80

Animal Chatter

Unscramble the letters and the name of each animal. the correct animal sound in each.

squeak   baa   gobble   moo   quack   meow   roar

oiln — *lion* — roar

emuos — *mouse* — squeak

cdku — *duck* — quack

pehse — *sheep* — baa

ekyurt — *turkey* — gobble

wco — *cow* — moo

tnitke — *kitten* — meow

Page 81

Size Search

Circle each size word. Write the correct number by each picture. Color each picture the correct color.

1. a long brown snake.
2. a little, red heart.
3. a tall green tree.
4. a large blue house.
5. a small orange gift.
6. a short yellow pencil.
7. a big, purple tent.

4
6
3
7
1
2
5

Page 82

Confection Perfection

Cut out the pictures of the candy at the bottom of the page. Paste the pictures to correctly continue the pattern in each row.

Page 83

Roaring Roller-Coaster Rides

Cut out the roller coaster cars at the bottom of the page. Paste them to correctly continue the pattern on each track.

Page 84

Strawberry Stack-Up

Farmers grow ripe, red strawberries for everyone to eat. Before taking the strawberries to the stores, the farmers put them in small baskets.

Look at the pattern of the baskets in each row. Draw the correct number of strawberries in the baskets to continue each pattern.

Page 85

Stringing It Along

Complete each pattern. Color the ♥ red and the ♡ pink.

Page 86

Special Hearts for a Special Friend

Look at the picture carefully.

How many hearts were used to draw the cat? __23__

Draw and color a picture of an animal using only heart shapes.

Pictures will vary.

Page 87

Animal Action

Find the shapes and color the picture using the code.

○ red   □ blue   ▭ yellow
△ green   ◇ orange   ⬭ black

Page 88

Cabin to Capitol

Abraham Lincoln was the 16th president of the United States. He was born in a log cabin. Many people lived in log cabins at that time.

Look at this picture of a log cabin. How many of each of the different shapes can you find in the picture?

How many △ 's? _3_   How many ▱ 's? _6_
How many □ 's? _9_   Draw and color a door.

Page 89

Mask Make-Up

Masks have been made by people for many years. In some countries, the actors in plays wear masks. Masks can be made from wood, metal, paper, cloth, or even foil. They can be painted with a design or a face. Color the mask by using the color code.

○ red   □ orange   △ yellow   □ blue

Page 90

Animal Shapes

Color:
squares — green
rectangles — yellow
circles — red
triangles — blue

Page 91

"Squaring" Off

Square dancing is a kind of folk dancing. The name of the dance comes from the shape the group of dancers form when they begin the dance – a square. As they dance, they form other shapes.

Look at the shapes and answer the questions.

How many ☐'s can you find?
_5_

One pattern the dancers form is called "a star." Each person puts one arm into the middle of the square. The square is cut into △'s.

How many △'s can you find?
_16_

Page 92

Rainbow-Colored Numbers

Color: 1's—red
2's—blue
3's—yellow
4's—green
5's—orange

Page 93

One Beautiful Butterfly

Color: 6's—purple
7's—yellow
8's—black
9's—orange
10's—brown

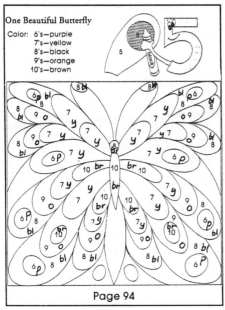

Page 94

Clown Count

Color the 🎈's:

1 - blue   2 - orange   3 - yellow   4 - green
5 - purple   6 - brown
7 - red   8 - black   9 - blue   10 - purple

Color clown, too!

Page 95

Wintry Ride

Count each set of bears. Draw a line from each set to the sled that has the correct number.

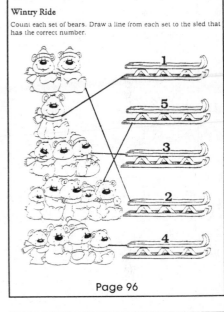

Page 96

Pack a Snack

Count each set of sandwiches. Draw a line from each set to the backpack that has the correct number.

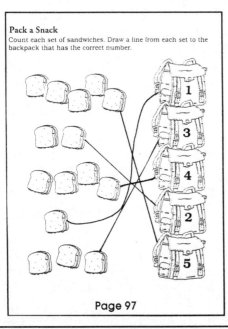

Page 97

Sheepish Shepherd

Count the sheep on each hill. Then write that number on each tree.

Page 98

Number Express

Number the train.

Draw a line from the word to the number.

seven
two
five
nine
six
four
one
three
eight

Color train cars.   one-red   three-green   five-orange
two-blue   four-yellow   six-brown

Page 99

299

Daily Learning Drills Grade 1

Beach Blanket Numbers
Count. Use code to color answers.

1—blue   4—red   7—purple
2—yellow   5—orange 8—gray
3—green   6—brown 9—black

Page 100

School Scene

How many?

(bird)	7
(cloud)	6
(tree)	9

(tulip)	8
(leaves)	3
(hills)	5

(slide)	1
(window)	4
(tree)	2

Page 101

Take an Animal Count!
Count the zoo animals in each box. Match the number to the correct number word by drawing a line to it. One is done for you.

four
eight
one
ten
seven
two
six
three
nine
five

Page 102

Connect the Dots
Join the dots in order.
Color the surprise.

Page 103

More Dot-to-Dot Fun
Connect the dots.

Page 104

Happy Hikers
Hike your way to camp. Trace a path through the maze by counting from 1 to 10 in the correct order. Color the picture.

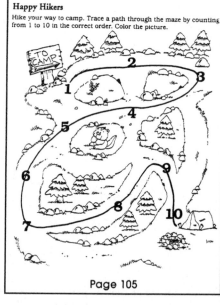

Page 105

Two for the Pool
Counting by 2's, write the numbers to 50 in the waterdrops. Start at the top of the slide and go down.

Page 106

I'm Counting on You
Write and count by 2's.

2	4	6	8	10	12	14	16	18	20

Write and count by 5's.

5	10	15	20	25	30	35	40	45	50

Connect the dots by 2's.

Connect the dots by 5's.

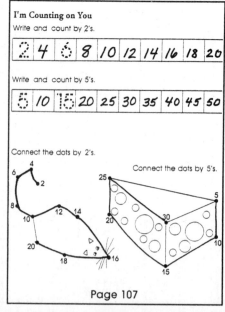

Page 107

Count the Cookie Clues
Find out what holds something crumbly, but good! Counting by 5's, connect the dots in order. Start with 5. Color the picture.

Page 108

Desert Trek

As you count by 10's, color each canteen with the number you say to lead the camel to the watering hole.

Caterpillar Count

Circle numbers counting by twos.

Count by 2's.

2 4 6 8 10 12 14 16

Put △ around numbers counting by fives.

Count by 5's.

5 10 15 20 25 30 35 40

Put ☐ around numbers counting by 10's.

Count by 10's.

10 20 30 40 50 60 70 80

Largest and Smallest

In the shapes, circle the smallest number. Draw a square around the largest number.

Barking Up a Tree

Use counters. Trace or draw each set you make. Then, write how many in all.

How many?	How many more?	How many in all?
3	2	5
2	1	3
4	3	7
1	6	7

Think of a story for this picture. Write how many in all.

5 in all

How Many in All?

2 + 2 = 4   2
              + 2
              ___
                4

Write an addition sentence and a vertical fact for each picture story. Find how many in all.

3 + 1 = 4   3
               + 1
               ___
                 4

2 + 3 = 5   2
               + 3
               ___
                 5

4 + 3 = 7   4
               + 3
               ___
                 7

2 + 6 = 8   2
               + 6
               ___
                 8

5 + 3 = 8   5
               + 3
               ___
                 8

2 + 5 = 7   2
               + 5
               ___
                 7

Addition Using Counters

Example   2 + 1 = 3

Use counters to add.

2 + 1 = ?

Put in 2.   Put in 1 more.

How many counters are there in all? 3

So, 2 + 1 = 3. The number that tells how many in all is called the **sum**. The sum of 2 + 1 is 3.

Use counters to find each sum.

2 + 4 = 6   5 + 2 = 7

3 + 3 = 6   3 + 4 = 7

Prehistoric Picture Problems

Circle the picture which matches the number sentence.

1. 1 + 2 = 3
2. 2 + 3 = 5
3. 4 + 2 = 6
4. 5 + 1 = 6
5. 3 + 4 = 7
6. 6 + 1 = 7

Alien Problems

Look at the pictures and finish the number sentences.

1. 2 + 3 = 5
2. 1 + 7 = 8
3. 4 + 3 = 7
4. 5 + 0 = 5
5. 3 + 3 = 6
6. 4 + 5 = 9

Bear Necessities: How Many More Are Needed?

Draw in the missing pictures and finish the number sentences.

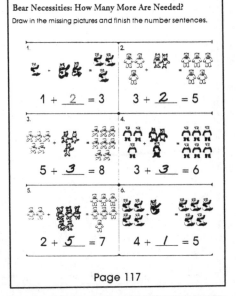

1. 1 + 2 = 3
2. 3 + 2 = 5
3. 5 + 3 = 8
4. 3 + 3 = 6
5. 2 + 5 = 7
6. 4 + 1 = 5

The Missing Chickens
Draw in the missing pictures and finish the number sentences.

1. _1_ + 2 = 3
2. _3_ + 3 = 6
3. 5 + _2_ = 7
4. _2_ + 3 = 5
5. _4_ + 4 = 8
6. 7 + _1_ = 8

Page 118

How Many Robots in All?
Look at the pictures and finish the number sentences.

1. 2 + 4 = 6
2. 3 + 5 = 8
3. 4 + 3 = 7
4. 4 + 1 = 5
5. 2 + 5 = 7
6. 4 + 4 = 8

Page 119

How Many Rabbits?
Look at the pictures and finish the number sentences.

1. 1 + 1 = 2
2. 3 + 6 = 9
3. 6 + 1 = 7
4. 3 + 4 = 7
5. 4 + 5 = 9
6. 2 + 3 = 5

Page 120

Bee Addition
3 + 1 =
Add. Use code to color each bee.   2—red   4—blue
3—yellow   5—green

1 + 2 = yellow
2 + 3 = 5 green
3 + 2 = 5 green
3 + 1 = 4 blue
1 + 1 = 2 red
2 + 2 = 4 blue
2 + 1 = 3 yellow
1 + 3 = 4 blue

Page 121

Lumberjack Facts
Add.
If the answer equals **1**, color the space **red**.
If the answer equals **2**, color the space **yellow**.
If the answer equals **3**, color the space **black**.
If the answer equals **4**, color the space **blue**.
If the answer equals **5**, color the space **brown**.
If the answer equals **6**, color the space **green**.

Page 122

Creature Count

5 + 1 = 6

4 + 6 = 10   1 + 9 = 10
7 + 1 = 8   7 + 3 = 10
5 + 2 = 7   6 + 1 = 7
8 + 2 = 10   3 + 5 = 8
6 + 3 = 9   6 + 2 = 8
4 + 5 = 9   1 + 7 = 8

Page 123

Beary Good
Put counters on each bear to show the addition. Write the sums.

3 + 2 = 5   5 + 0 = 5   1 + 6 = 7   4 + 2 = 6

6	3	2	5	7	0
+1	+4	+3	+2	+1	+2
7	7	5	7	8	2

8	4	3	2	3	6
+0	+5	+6	+6	+5	+2
8	9	9	8	8	8

Page 124

Animal Addition

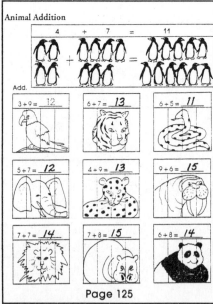

4 + 7 = 11

Add.

3 + 9 = 12   6 + 7 = 13   6 + 5 = 11
5 + 7 = 12   4 + 9 = 13   9 + 6 = 15
7 + 7 = 14   7 + 8 = 15   6 + 8 = 14

Page 125

Add the Apples
Match.

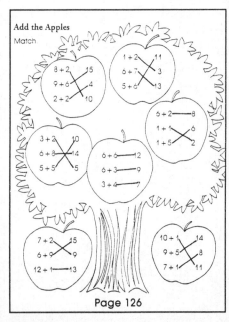

8 + 2 — 15
9 + 6 — 4
2 + 2 — 10

1 + 2 — 11
6 + 7 — 3
5 + 6 — 13

6 + 2 — 8
1 + 1 — 6
1 + 6 — 8

3 + 2 — 10
6 + 8 — 14
5 + 5 — 5

6 + 6 — 12
6 + 3 — 9
3 + 4 — 9

7 + 2 — 15
6 + 9 — 9
12 + 1 — 13

10 + 1 — 14
9 + 5 — 8
7 + 1 — 11

Page 126

What's the Difference?

Example $5 - 2 = \underline{?}$

Use counters to subtract.

Put in 5. Take away 2.

How many counters are left? $\underline{3}$

So, $5 - 2 = 3$. The number that tells how many are left is called the **difference**. The difference of $5 - 2$ is 3.

Use counters to find each difference.

$6 - 3 = \underline{3}$ $5 - 1 = \underline{4}$

$5 - 3 = \underline{2}$ $4 - 2 = \underline{2}$

Page 127

Counting Kittens

Use counters. Make a set, then take away. Write how many are left.

$\underline{3}$ are left.

Put in 4. Take away 1.

$\underline{3}$ are left.

Put in 5. Take away 2.

$\underline{5}$ are left.

Put in 6. Take away 1.

$\underline{4}$ are left.

Put in 7. Take away 3.

Think of a story for this picture. Write how many are left. $\underline{3}$ are left.

Page 128

Transportation Problems

Circle the picture which matches the number sentence. Then finish the number sentence.

1. $4 - 1 = \underline{3}$ 2. $6 - 2 = \underline{4}$

3. $5 - 3 = \underline{2}$ 4. $7 - 3 = \underline{4}$

5. $5 - 2 = \underline{3}$ 6. $7 - 5 = \underline{2}$

Page 129

Sea Creature Subtraction

Look at the pictures and finish the number sentences.

1. How many 🐬's are left?
$4 - 4 = \underline{0}$

2. How many 🐟's are left?
$6 - 2 = \underline{4}$

3. How many 🐟's are left?
$7 - 3 = \underline{4}$

4. How many 🐟's are left?
$6 - 5 = \underline{1}$

5. How many 🐟's are left?
$8 - 3 = \underline{5}$

6. How many 🐟's are left?
$5 - 2 = \underline{3}$

Page 130

Nutty Subtraction

Count the nuts.
Write answer on blank.
Circle problems with same answer.

Page 131

Robins and Worms

$3 - 2 = 1$

$\begin{array}{r} 3 \\ -2 \\ \hline 1 \end{array}$

$5 - 1 = \underline{4}$ $3 - 1 = \underline{2}$ $5 - 2 = \underline{3}$
$4 - 1 = \underline{3}$ $2 - 1 = \underline{1}$ $4 - 2 = \underline{2}$
$3 - 2 = \underline{1}$ $4 - 3 = \underline{1}$ $5 - 3 = \underline{2}$

Subtract. Use code to color worms.   1–red   3–yellow
2–orange   4–brown

$\begin{array}{r} 5 \\ -1 \\ \hline \end{array}$ ④ $\begin{array}{r} 4 \\ -2 \\ \hline \end{array}$ ② $\begin{array}{r} 5 \\ -2 \\ \hline \end{array}$ ③
brown   orange   yellow

$\begin{array}{r} 3 \\ -1 \\ \hline \end{array}$ ② $\begin{array}{r} 4 \\ -3 \\ \hline \end{array}$ ① $\begin{array}{r} 5 \\ -3 \\ \hline \end{array}$ ②
orange   red   orange

$\begin{array}{r} 2 \\ -1 \\ \hline \end{array}$ ① $\begin{array}{r} 4 \\ -1 \\ \hline \end{array}$ ③ $\begin{array}{r} 3 \\ -2 \\ \hline \end{array}$ ①
red   yellow   red

Page 132

"Berry" Tasty

Subtract.
If the answer is **0**, color the space **green**.
If the answer is **1**, color the space **brown**.
If the answer is **2**, color the space **blue**.
If the answer is **3**, color the space **purple**.
If the answer is **4**, color the space **black**.
If the answer is **5**, color the space **pink**.

Page 133

Bubbly Baths

Subtract. Write each answer on the rubber duck.

Page 134

Fewer Fruits

$9 - 2 = 7$ $\begin{array}{r} 7 \\ -1 \\ \hline 6 \end{array}$

Subtract. Use code to color.   6–orange   9–green
7–red   10–purple
8–yellow

$11 - 1 = \underline{10}$ $\begin{array}{r} 9 \\ -1 \\ \hline 8 \end{array}$ $8 - 1 = \underline{7}$
purple   yellow   red

$10 - 4 = \underline{6}$ $\begin{array}{r} 9 \\ -2 \\ \hline 7 \end{array}$ $\begin{array}{r} 10 \\ -1 \\ \hline 9 \end{array}$
orange   red   green

$10 - 2 = \underline{8}$ $11 - 2 = \underline{9}$ $\begin{array}{r} 10 \\ -3 \\ \hline 7 \end{array}$
yellow   green   red

Page 135

Daily Learning Drills Grade 1

Sweet Treats

Count the candy.
Write number on blank.
Circle problems with same answer.

Page 136

A Whale of a Job!

For each problem, put the number of counters needed in the water, then take away by sliding the numbers into the whale's mouth. Then, count how many counters are left in the water to find the difference.

$\frac{7}{-4}$ $\frac{9}{-7}$ $\frac{6}{-4}{2}$ $\frac{5}{-2}{3}$ $\frac{8}{-3}{5}$

$\frac{9}{-3}{6}$ $\frac{6}{-3}{3}$ $\frac{7}{-5}{2}$ $\frac{8}{-2}{6}$ $\frac{5}{-1}{4}$

$8 - 4 = 4$ $6 - 2 = 4$ $7 - 4 = 3$

Page 137

Hop Along Numbers

Use the number line to **count back**.

8, _7_, _6_   6, _5_, _4_

5, _4_, _3_   7, _6_, _5_, _4_

Use the number line to count back to find each difference.

Example: $9 - 2 = 2$ Start with 9. Count back 2.

9, _8_, _7_ $9 - 2 = 7$

$7 - 3 = 4$ $6 - 2 = 4$
7, _6_, _5_, _4_   6, _5_, _4_

$8 - 1 = 7$ $7 - 2 = 5$
8, _7_   7, _6_, _5_

Page 138

Crayon Count

Count crayons. Write number on blank.
Circle problems that name answer.

Page 139

Turtle Math—Take It Slow

Color answer:
2—red
3—blue
4—yellow
5—green

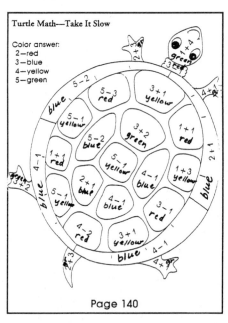

Page 140

It's Show Time

It's time for Packy and Dermit to perform. Look at the problems. Write + or – on each peanut to make the problem correct. Then trace a path from peanut to peanut, connecting each elephant to the correct stool. For Packy, connect all of the + problems. For Dermit, connect all of the – problems.

Page 141

Puppy Problems

Look at the pictures and finish the number sentences.

1. $5 \oplus 6 = 11$ 2. $11 \ominus 4 = 7$

3. $12 \ominus 7 = 5$ 4. $7 \oplus 6 = 13$

5. $5 \oplus 5 = 10$ 6. $8 \oplus 6 = 14$

Page 142

Calling All Cats

Look at the pictures and finish the number sentences.

1. How many ❄'s are there in all?   2. How many ❄'s are there in all?
$7 \ominus 4 = 11$ $6 \oplus 8 = 14$

3. How many ♪'s are there in all?   4. How many ♪'s are left?
$11 \oplus 2 = 13$ $13 \ominus 7 = 6$

5. How many ♪'s are left?   6. How many ♪'s are left?
$9 \ominus 6 = 3$ $12 \ominus 8 = 4$

Page 143

What Was the Question?

Draw a line under the question that matches the picture. Then finish the number sentence.

1. How many 🐸's are there in all?
   How many 🐸's are left?
   $11 - 7 = 4$

2. How many 🐢's are there in all?
   How many 🐢's are left?
   $4 + 5 = 9$

3. How many 🍄's are there in all?
   How many 🍄's are left?
   $8 - 3 = 5$

4. How many 🍄's are there in all?
   How many 🍄's are left?
   $10 - 4 = 6$

5. How many 🦋's are there in all?
   How many 🦋's are left?
   $5 + 6 = 11$

6. How many 🐝's are there in all?
   How many 🐝's are left?
   $8 + 4 = 12$

Page 144

Sunny Day Delight

Draw a line under the question that matches the picture.
Then finish the number sentence.

1. How many 🍦's are there in all?
How many 🍦's are left?
$6 + 6 = 12$

2. How many 🍦's are there in all?
How many 🍦's are left?
$13 - 4 = 9$

3. How many 🍦's are there in all?
How many 🍦's are left?
$9 + 5 = 14$

4. How many 🍦's are there in all?
How many 🍦's are left?
$13 - 5 = 8$

5. How many 🍦's are there in all?
How many 🍦's are left?
$7 + 7 = 14$

6. How many 🍦's are there in all?
How many 🍦's are left?
$9 - 5 = 4$

Page 145

Fishing for Answers

$5 > 3$
5 is greater than 3

$3 < 5$
3 is less than 5.

Fill in number line.

| 1 | 2 | 3 | 4 | 5 | 6 | 7 | 8 | 9 | 10 |

$3 > 2$ $3 < 4$

Write > or <. Use number line to help you.

5 $>$ 2   1 $<$ 7   1 $<$ 4   8 $>$ 5
3 $<$ 4   9 $>$ 3   8 $>$ 7   2 $<$ 4
6 $>$ 5   5 $>$ 3   5 $>$ 7   3 $<$ 5
7 $>$ 3   7 $>$ 6   2 $<$ 8   4 $>$ 2

Page 146

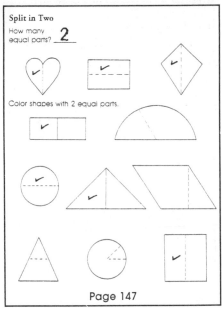

Split in Two

How many equal parts? **2**

Color shapes with 2 equal parts.

Page 147

Thirds

How many equal parts? **3**

Color shapes with 3 equal parts.

Page 148

Fourths

How many equal parts? **4**

Color shapes with 4 equal parts.

Page 149

Fractions Review

How many equal parts?

2   3   4   4   2

Color shapes with 2 equal parts red,
3 parts blue and 4 parts green.

Page 150

A Race!

first   fourth
second   fifth   sixth
third   seventh

Write the correct word to tell where each runner placed in the race.

1. sixth
2. fifth
3. seventh
4. fourth
5. first
6. third
7. second

Flip Fun! Draw a prize you would like to receive for winning a race.

Page 151

Flags First

Color the ninth flag red.
Write O on the second flag.
Color the eighth flag blue.
Write D on the fourth flag.
Color the sixth flag yellow.
Write G on the first flag.
Color the tenth flag purple.
Write O on the third flag.
Color the seventh flag green.
Color the fifth flag orange.

Page 152

Balls of All Kinds

1 2 3 4 5

Color second ball brown.
Color sixth ball yellow.
Color fourth ball orange.
Color first ball black.
Color third ball blue.
Color fifth ball green.
Color seventh ball purple.
Color eighth ball pink.

Page 153

Daily Learning Drills Grade 1

Sir Circle Counts Coins!

Count the coins. Circle the set with more money.

Example		
12¢ 21¢	22¢ 16¢	21¢ 13¢
19¢ 30¢	27¢ 22¢	16¢ 23¢
32¢ 37¢	29¢ 24¢	14¢ 15¢

Page 163

Watch the Time

Show the class how to put numbers on the watch and draw watch hands. Students then color and cut out the watch. Tape it to fit the wrist.

1 2 3
4 5 6
7 8 9
10 11 12

Page 164

Hickory Dickory Dock

What time is it?

4 o'clock   9 o'clock   6 o'clock

2 o'clock   10 o'clock   8 o'clock

3 o'clock   11 o'clock   7 o'clock

1 o'clock   5 o'clock   12 o'clock

Page 165

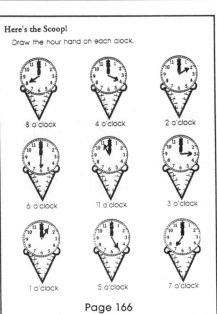

Here's the Scoop!

Draw the hour hand on each clock.

8 o'clock   4 o'clock   2 o'clock

6 o'clock   11 o'clock   3 o'clock

1 o'clock   5 o'clock   7 o'clock

Page 166

Timely News

Cut out the newspapers at the bottom of the page. Paste each newspaper below the correct clock.

3:30   12:30   5:30   6:30
10:30   (blank)   8:30   4:30
7:30   1:30   11:30   9:30

Page 167

Who "Nose" These Times?

Write the time under each clock. Color the noses.

4:00   4:30

9:00   9:30   2:00   2:30

5:00   5:30   8:00   8:30

1:00   1:30   11:00   11:30

Page 168

Sock Clocks

Draw the hands on the sock clocks.

1:30   7:00   4:30

10:00   3:30   9:30

4:00   2:30   6:00

Page 169

It's Time to Eat!

Follow the directions below the clock.

1. Draw a yellow banana at 7:00.
2. Draw a hamburger at 12:00.
3. Draw a red apple at 10:00.
4. Draw a fried egg at 6:00.
5. Draw a hot dog at 11:00.
6. Draw an orange carrot at 1:00.
7. Draw a piece of pizza at 5:00.
8. Draw a donut at 9:00.
9. Draw an ice cream cone with three flavors at 2:00.
10. Draw an ear of corn at 4:00.
11. Draw a chicken leg at 8:00.
12. Draw your favorite food at 3:00.

Page 170

What a Day!

The camp director needs help planning activities for tomorrow afternoon. Read the list carefully. Then use the times to number the activities in the order they will happen.

8 5:30 p.m. Supper
7 4:30 p.m. Crafts
4 1:30 p.m. Baseball game
6 3:00 p.m. Swimming
5 2:30 p.m. Water Safety
3 2:00 p.m. Walk in the woods
9 6:30 p.m. Boating
2 12:30 p.m. First Aid Lesson
1 12:00 noon Lunch
10 7:30 p.m. Campfire

Which activity would you most enjoy doing? Why?
Answers will vary.

Which activity would you least enjoy doing? Why?
Answers will vary.

Page 171

307   Daily Learning Drills Grade 1

It's About Time

There are many ways we measure time. A year is made of 365 days. A week has seven days. A day has 24 hours. An hour is made of 60 minutes. A minute is made of 60 seconds. A second goes very quickly. Can you blink your eyes in one second?

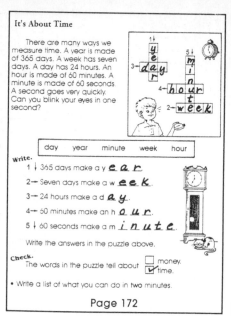

| day | year | minute | week | hour |

Write.

1 ↓ 365 days make a y **e a r**

2 → Seven days make a w **e e k**

3 → 24 hours make a d **a y**

4 → 60 minutes make an h **o u r**

5 ↓ 60 seconds make a m **i n u t e**

Write the answers in the puzzle above.

Check.
The words in the puzzle tell about ☐ money. ☑ time.

• Write a list of what you can do in two minutes.

Page 172

Fun Days

There are seven days in a week. Saturday and Sunday are the weekend days. You go to school the other five days. Which day do you like best?

DAYS
Sunday
Monday
Tuesday
Wednesday
Thursday
Friday
Saturday

How many days are in a week?

six (seven) ten

Which two days make a weekend?

Saturday	*Saturday*
Thursday	*Sunday*
Sunday	

____ the five days you go to school.

• Draw and color what you do on a weekend.

Page 173

Hmm, What Month Is It?

There are twelve months in a year. The first month is January. The last month is December. Some months have 31 days. Some months have 30 days. February is the shortest month with 28 days. Can you name the months of the year?

4 April
10 October
12 December
7 July
3 March
1 January
5 May
9 September
6 June
2 February
8 August
11 November

Check.
How many months are in a year? ☐ five ☐ nine ☑ twelve

Write.
January   *December*
first month   last month

Circle.
Yes or No
Some months have 30 days.   (Yes) No
Some months have 31 days.   (Yes) No
February is the longest month.   Yes (No)
February has 28 days.   (Yes) No

Write 1-12 in the ☐'s to put the months in order.

• Write the names of the twelve months in the correct order.

Page 174

How Did You Do That?

You use many parts of your body to do even the simplest activities.

Read each activity and write the body parts you would use to do that activity.

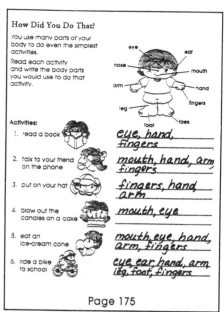

eye   ear   nose   mouth   arm   hand   fingers   leg   foot   toes

Activities:

1. read a book — *eye, hand, fingers*

2. talk to your friend on the phone — *mouth, hand, arm, fingers*

3. put on your hat — *fingers, hand, arm*

4. blow out the candles on a cake — *mouth, eye*

5. eat an ice-cream cone — *mouth, eye, hand, arm, fingers*

6. ride a bike to school — *eye, ear, hand, arm, leg, foot, fingers*

Page 175

Body Buddies

Follow the numbers to print a word that is part of your body. Then color each part.

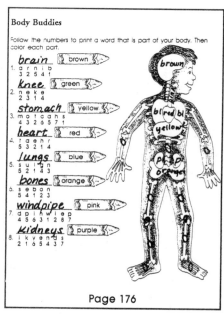

brain — brown
1. a r n i b / 3 2 5 4 1

knee — green
2. n e k e / 2 3 1 4

stomach — yellow
3. m o t c a h s / 4 3 2 6 5 7 1

heart — red
4. t a e h r / 5 3 2 1 4

lungs — blue
5. s u l g n / 5 2 1 4 3

bones — orange
6. s e b o n / 5 4 1 2 3

windpipe — pink
7. d p i h w i e p / 4 5 6 1 2 8 7

kidneys — purple
8. i k v e n d s / 2 1 6 5 4 3 7

brown
bl red bl
yellow
p p
orange

Page 176

It Makes Sense to Me

Our five senses help us understand and make "sense" of our world. Look at each group of pictures. Decide which sense (see, hear, smell, taste, or feel) is used for most items in each group of pictures. Write the sense on the line below each group. Then put an X on the one picture that does not belong in each group.

hear   *feel*

taste

smell   *see*

Page 177

Outfitted for Health

Read the phrases in the Word Bank. Write only the **good** health habits on the lines.

Word Bank	Take a bath.	Eat a lot of sweets.	Stay up all night.
	Drink water.	Get plenty of sleep.	Keep cuts clean.
	Sit all day.	Never wash your hands.	Brush your teeth.
	Exercise.	Eat healthy foods.	

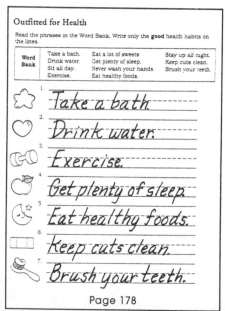

1. *Take a bath.*

2. *Drink water.*

3. *Exercise.*

4. *Get plenty of sleep.*

5. *Eat healthy foods.*

6. *Keep cuts clean.*

7. *Brush your teeth.*

Page 178

Exercise!

Do you like to exercise? Exercise is good for you. Walking and running are good ways to exercise. So are swimming and biking. Some people like to do push-ups, sit-ups and jumping jacks. Exercise can help you feel good. It can make your body stronger, too. What is your favorite kind of exercise?

Unscramble.
Exercise is good for you.
s r E e o x i e e
7 4 1 5 2 6 3 8

Write.
walking
swimming
biking
running

swimming   *walking*
running   *biking*

Check.
What do some people do for exercise?
☑ push-ups ☐ sleep ☑ jumping jacks ☑ sit-ups

Circle.
Yes or No
Exercise can help you feel good.   (Yes) No
Exercise is very easy.   Yes (No)
Exercise can make your body stronger. (Yes) No

• Draw a picture of you exercising.

Page 179

Pyramiding Foods

Read the names of the foods in the Word Bank. Write the words on the lines under the correct food group.

carrots cherries
chicken cheese
fish ham cake
lettuce bagel oranges
pears rolls beans
toast pie yogurt
candy cottage
bar cheese

dairy
cheese
yogurt
cottage cheese

meats
ham
fish
chicken

fruits
pears
oranges
cherries

sweets
cake
pie
candy bar

vegetables
carrots
lettuce
beans

grains
bagel
rolls
toast

Page 180

Leaf Shapes

All leaves are not the same. They have different shapes. There are four common shapes.

Draw a line to match the leaf with its shape.

Find some leaves outside.
Try to match them to the shapes.

Page 181

Tree Parts

Trees have three main parts. They are the trunk, the roots, and the leaves. Each part has a special job. Each part helps the tree.
Cut out the name of each part.
Cut out the job of each part.
Paste them on the picture.
Color the tree.

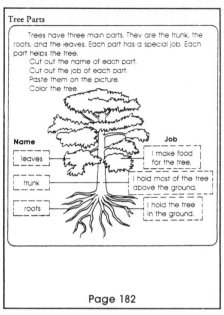

Name

leaves

trunk

roots

Job

I make food for the tree.

I hold most of the tree above the ground.

I hold the tree in the ground.

Page 182

Leaf Study

Put a leaf under the box on this paper. Rub the paper with the side of your crayon. Use the ruler at the bottom to measure your leaf.

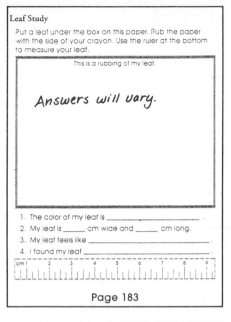

This is a rubbing of my leaf.

Answers will vary.

1. The color of my leaf is _____
2. My leaf is _____ cm wide and _____ cm long.
3. My leaf feels like _____
4. I found my leaf _____

Page 183

Food Factories

Green leaves are like little factories. They make food for the tree. Leaves need sunshine, air, and water to make food.

Leaves change in the fall. They lose their green color. Then they cannot make food for the tree.

Draw a leaf.
This leaf can make food.
Color it green.
Write the correct word.

Draw another leaf.
This leaf cannot make food.
Color it with pretty fall colors.

green yellow

Food is made by __*green*__ leaves.

shade sunshine

Leaves need __*sunshine*__ to make food.

can cannot

Leaves __*cannot*__ make food in the fall.

Page 184

My Leaf Collection

Attach a leaf and fill in the blanks.
Teacher: Provide each student with three or more copies of this page so booklets can be made.

Answers will vary.

Tree _____
Location _____
Date _____

Page 185

From Acorn to Mighty Oak

Some trees drop their seeds in the spring. Other trees drop their seeds in the fall. The seeds grow up. Do you know what they grow up to be?

Show how the acorn grows into a mighty oak tree. Write first, second, or third under the pictures to put them in order. Color the pictures.

__*first*__   __*third*__   __*second*__

Finish the story.
I am a little acorn. One day _____

__*Stories will vary.*__

Page 186

Plant Parts

A plant has many parts. Each part has a special job.

Word Bank   roots   stem
              flower   leaf

Label the parts of the plant.

__*flower*__
__*stem*__
__*leaf*__
__*roots*__

Draw a line from the plant part to its job.

I make the seeds.
I make food for the plant.
I take water from the roots to the leaves.
I hold the plant in the ground.

Color the roots red.
Color the stem yellow.
Color the leaves green.
Color the flower your favorite color.

Page 187

Growing Words

Write each word on the line below the correct picture.

pumpkin   seed   sprout   flower   plant

__*flower*__   __*plant*__

__*sprout*__

__*pumpkin*__   __*seed*__

Page 188

Edible Plant Parts

We eat many plant parts. Sometimes we eat just the fruit. Sometimes we eat just the leaves. We also might eat the stem, the root, or the seed.

Draw a line from the picture to the name of the plant part.
Color the plant part.

Stem

Leaf

Root

Seed

Fruit

Page 189

Daily Learning Drills Grade 1

Plant It Right!

Mr. Right and Mr. Wrong planted gardens. Mr. Right planted his garden in the sun. Mr. Wrong planted his garden in the shade. Both of them gave their gardens love and care.

Draw what Mr. Right's garden will look like.

Pictures will vary— tall, healthy plants.

Draw what Mr. Wrong's garden will look like.

Pictures will vary— small plants.

Page 190

Water, Please!

Mrs. Right planted her flower seeds last week. She planted them in the sun. She gave her flowers water.

Draw what Mrs. Right's flowers will look like.

Mrs. Wrong planted her flower seeds last week. She planted them in the sun. But she forgot to give them water.

Draw what Mrs. Wrong's flowers will look like.

Pictures will vary.

Page 191

All in the Family

Put an X on the animal that does not belong.

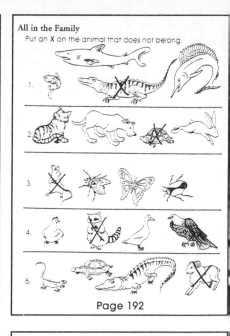

1.
2.
3.
4.
5.

Page 192

Animals on the Go

How do these animals move?
Write **walk**, **fly** or **swim**.

swim   walk   fly

swim   walk   fly

fly   walk   swim

Page 193

Pond Community

Many animals make their homes in a pond community, but some of the animals in this picture do not belong.

Draw an X on the animals that do **not** belong.

Page 194

Grassland Community

Many animals make their homes in a grassland community, but some of the animals in this picture do not belong.

Draw an X on the animals that do **not** belong.

Page 195

Ocean Community

Many animals make their homes in an ocean community, but some of the animals in this picture do not belong.

Draw an X on the animals that do **not** belong.

Page 196

Forest Community

Many animals make their homes in a forest community, but some of the animals in this picture do not belong.

Draw an X on the animals that do **not** belong.

Page 197

Animals at Home

Did you ever see a fish living in a tree? Of course you didn't! Fish live in the water. Help the animals find their homes.

Cut out each animal. Paste it on its home. Color the picture.

robin

bee

squirrel

fish

Page 198

Where's My Baby?

Match the adult animal to the baby animal!

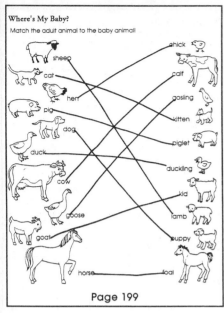

sheep → chick
cat → calf
hen → gosling
pig → kitten
dog → piglet
duck → duckling
cow → kid
goose → lamb
goat → puppy
horse → foal

Page 199

Feathered Friends

Name the parts of the bird.

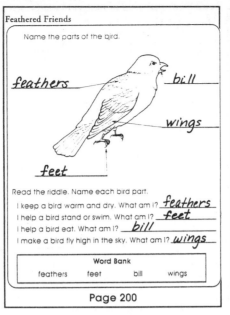

feathers   bill   wings   feet

Read the riddle. Name each bird part.

I keep a bird warm and dry. What am I? __feathers__
I help a bird stand or swim. What am I? __feet__
I help a bird eat. What am I? __bill__
I make a bird fly high in the sky. What am I? __wings__

Word Bank			
feathers	feet	bill	wings

Page 200

My Bird List

Bird watchers keep a list of all the different kinds of birds they have seen. They also keep track of the date and location. Begin a list of your own using the chart below.

Bird	Date	Location

__Lists will vary.__

Page 201

I Slither and Crawl

Do the puzzle about reptiles.
Color only the reptiles.

(crossword) scales / turtle / snake / old / egg

Across
2. A reptile's skin has __scales__
5. A __snake__ is a reptile with no legs.

Down
1. A __turtle__ is a reptile with a hard shell on its back.
3. Reptiles are __cold__ -blooded animals.
4. Baby reptiles hatch from __eggs__

Word Bank				
eggs	cold	scales	snake	turtle

Page 202

A Reptile Riddle

Circle the animal that does not belong in the group. Print the letters beside the circled words in the spaces below to find the answer to the riddle.

Birds
1. L robin
   N bluebird
   I (cow)
   J crow

Insects
2. L (snake)
   A ladybug
   N wasp
   T bee

Dogs
3. B collie
   I beagle
   S shepherd
   L (OX)

Reptiles
4. R snake
   I (horse)
   G turtle
   W alligator

Farm Animals
5. G (tiger)
   K pig
   O cow
   Y hen

Jungle Animals
6. J lion
   B cheetah
   U tiger
   A (rat)

Zoo Animals
7. M bear
   O giraffe
   T (dog)
   F zebra

Ocean Animals
8. H octopus
   T whale
   K shark
   O (camel)

Fish
9. R (raccoon)
   I perch
   V catfish
   L tuna

Riddle
What do you call a sick crocodile?

An __illigator__
1 2 3 4 5 6 7 8 9

Page 203

I'm Slippery and Cold

Do the puzzle about amphibians.
Color only the amphibians.

(crossword) eggs / cold / gills / skin / land

Down
1. Amphibian babies usually hatch from __eggs__
2. Amphibians are __cold__ -blooded animals.
4. Amphibians often have smooth, moist __skin__

Across
3. Amphibian babies breathe with either lungs or __gills__
5. Amphibians live in the water and on __land__

Word Bank				
land	gills	skin	eggs	cold

Page 204

From Mice to Whales

Do the puzzle about mammals.
Color only the mammals.

(crossword) warm / hair / milk / lungs / babies

Down
1. Mammals are __warm__ -blooded.
4. Mammals breathe with __lungs__

Across
2. A mammal's body is usually covered with __hair__
3. Mother mammals feed __milk__ to their babies.
5. Mammal's __babies__ are born alive.

Word Bank				
hair	babies	lungs	milk	warm

Page 205

Just Hanging Around

Bats like to fly at night. They sleep in the daytime. A bat sleeps by hanging upside down. Most bats live in trees and caves. Have you ever seen a bat?

night   noon

Bats like to fly at __night__

Bats sleep in the (daytime.)   room.

How do bats sleep?

Most bats live in:
☑ trees
☑ caves
☐ floor

the bats black.

• Draw and color a cave with sleeping bats in it.

Page 206

Crawling with Insects

Do the puzzle about insects.
Color only the insects.

(crossword) wings / skeleton / legs / three / eyes

Down
1. Insects have a hard outer __skeleton__
2. Many insects have two pairs of __wings__
5. Insects have simple and compound __eyes__

Across
3. Insects have three pairs of __legs__
4. Insects have __three__ main body sections.

Word Bank				
skeleton	legs	wings	three	eyes

Page 207

Daily Learning Drills Grade 1

Spinning Spiders

There are many kinds of spiders. Spiders have eight legs. They like to eat insects. Many spiders spin a web. The web is the spider's home. Have you ever seen a spider's web?

eight   four

Spiders have *eight* legs.

I spin a ~~week.~~ (web)
The web is my ~~kite.~~ (home)

What do spiders like to eat?
☑ Insects
☐ Jelly

8 black legs on this spider.
3 black spiders on the big web.

• Draw and color a spider and its web.

Page 208

Fish for Me

Do the puzzle about fish.
Color only the fish.

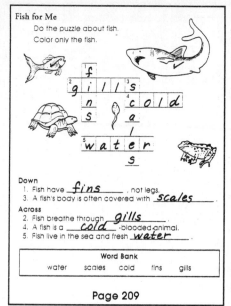

```
      f
  g i l l s
    n   c o l d
    s   a
        l
  w a t e r
        s
```

Down
1. Fish have *fins*, not legs.
3. A fish's body is often covered with *scales*

Across
2. Fish breathe through *gills*
4. A fish is a *cold*-blooded animal.
5. Fish live in the sea and fresh *water*

Word Bank
water   scales   cold   fins   gills

Page 209

"Hatch" Something Up

Many animals are hatched from eggs.
Read the clues. Then use the Word Bank to write the name of the correct animal on each egg.

alligator
I am a reptile.
I have big, sharp teeth.
I live near a river.

mud turtle
I live most of my life in water.
I eat tadpoles and water insects.
I can pull myself inside my shell.

duck
I have feathers.
I have webbed feet.
I swim in a pond.
I quack with my bill.

chick
I have feathers.
I live on a farm.
I have wings and make peeping sounds with my beak.

frog
I live near water.
I eat insects.
I have a tail when I hatch, but I lose it as I grow.
I can leap up to six feet.

Word Bank
snake   frog   mud turtle   chick   duck   alligator

Page 210

Butterfly – Part 1

Cut out the butterfly.
Cut out the egg.
Paste them on the milkweed leaf.

The butterfly lays one *egg* on a milkweed *leaf*

Page 211

Butterfly – Part 2

Cut out the caterpillar.
Paste it on the milkweed leaf.
Color the caterpillar black, white, and yellow.

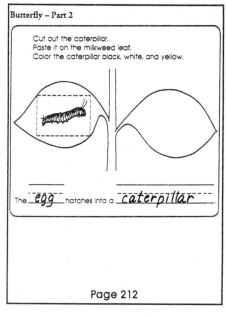

The *egg* hatches into a *caterpillar*

Page 212

Butterfly – Part 3

Cut out the caterpillar and its food.
Paste them on the milkweed plant.

The hungry caterpillar eats the *leaf*

The caterpillar is *growing*

Page 213

Butterfly – Part 4

Cut out the chrysalis.
Paste it in place.

The caterpillar is ready to *change*

It forms a pale *green* chrysalis.

Page 214

Butterfly – Part 5

Cut out the butterfly.
Paste it in place.

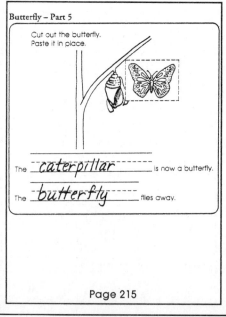

The *caterpillar* is now a butterfly.
The *butterfly* flies away.

Page 215

Metamorphosis

Show how the monarch changes.
Cut out the pictures.
Paste them in order.

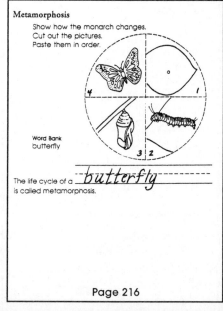

Word Bank
butterfly

The life cycle of a *butterfly* is called metamorphosis.

Page 216

Migration

Cut out the animals.
Paste them in place.

It is hard to find ___food___ in the winter.

It is hard to stay ___warm___ in the winter.

Some animals move to warmer places then.
This is called migration.

Page 217

Active Animals

Cut out the animals.
Paste them in place.

It is winter.
Deep snow covers the ground.

Some animals can find ___food___

Some animals can stay ___warm___

These animals stay active in winter.

Page 218

Storing Food

Cut out the beaver.
Paste him by the hole in the ice.
Trace the path to the beaver's lodge.

Some animals store food for ___winter___

The beaver stores food in his ___lodge___

Page 219

Hibernation

Cut out the fat woodchuck.
Paste him by his hole.
Trace the path to the
woodchuck's home.

Some animals hibernate in the winter.

The woodchuck grows a layer of ___fat___ in the fall.

His heartbeat goes ___down___. His temperature goes

___down___. He stays in his home while it is ___cold___.

Page 220

Animals in Winter

Cut out the animal.
Paste it in its place.
Write the animal's name.

This animal hibernates in the winter.

___woodchuck___

This animal migrates in the winter.

___bird___

This animal stays active in the winter.

___rabbit___

This animal stores food for the winter.

___beaver___

Page 221

Animal Homes

Follow the directions below to finish the picture.

1. Draw a fish in the lake.
2. Draw a whale in the ocean.
3. Draw a dog beside the river.
4. Draw a goat on the mountain.
5. Draw a bird on the island.
6. Now color the picture.

Page 222

Blooms and Birds

It is warm in the spring.
Flowers begin to bloom.
Trees have new leaves.
Birds make their nests and
lay eggs. Do you like to fly
a kite in the spring?

warm   last

It is ___warm___ in the spring.

What can you see in the spring?

What do birds do in the spring?

- [✔] Birds make nests.
- [✔] They lay eggs.
- [ ] They wash dishes.

• Draw and color a nest with four eggs in it.

Page 223

Fun in the Sun

Summer can be very
hot. It is the time when kids
are out of school. They have
fun playing with friends,
swimming to keep cool,
and sometimes going on
family picnics and vacations.

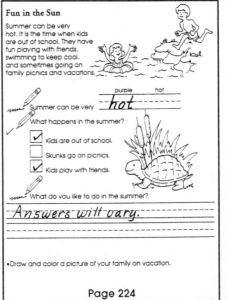

purple   hot

Summer can be very ___hot___

What happens in the summer?

- [✔] Kids are out of school.
- [ ] Skunks go on picnics.
- [✔] Kids play with friends.

What do you like to do in the summer?

___Answers will vary.___

• Draw and color a picture of your family on vacation.

Page 224

Autumn Leaves

The air gets cool in the
autumn. Kids go back to
school. Animals store food
for the winter. Leaves turn
red, yellow and orange. It is
a pretty time of the year.

time   cool

The air gets ___cool___ in the autumn.

What happens in the autumn?

- [✔] Kids go back to school.
- [✔] Animals store food.
- [ ] The air is very hot.

red   yellow   orange

• Draw and color an autumn tree.

Page 225

Winter Warm-ups

Winter can be cold and snowy. Animals stay near each other to keep warm. People wear coats, hats and Kids can make a snowman. It is fun to play in the snow.

Winter can be: ☑ cold
☑ snowy
☐ purple

like   warm

We try to stay _warm_

What do people wear in the winter?

gloves   hat   pan   coat

a black _____ on the _____

• Draw and color a snowman.

Page 226

The Four Seasons

1. Cut out and paste the season words on the correct boxes below.

2. Color the clothes for:
Fall – blue; Winter – red;
Spring – green; Summer – yellow

Winter   Spring

Summer   Fall

Page 227

Frederick's Furry Friends

Draw picture details of the four seasons around each of Frederick's furry friends. [...] the pictures and each mouse.

Pictures will vary.

Spring Mouse   Summer Mouse

Fall Mouse   Winter Mouse

Page 228

Magnetic Attraction

Draw a line from the magnet to each thing that it can pull.

Page 229

Sticky Hunt

What things will a magnet stick to?

Make lists of the things in your room that will and will not stick to a magnet. *Answers will vary.*

Magnets stick to:	Magnets do not stick to:

Caution: Do not try your magnet on these things.

TV   Computer disks
VCR   Cassette tapes
Computer   Video tapes
Radio   Credit cards
Tape recorder   Telephone

Page 230

Opposites Attract

Every magnet has a north pole and a south pole. When you hold two magnets together, this is what happens:

If a north pole and a south pole are next to each other, the magnets attract each other.

[S] → ← [S]

If two north poles or two south poles are next to each other, the magnets repel each other.

← [S   N] [N   S] →

Tell what each pair of magnets below will do. If the magnets will attract each other, color them red. If the magnets will repel each other, color them blue.

Page 231

Our Planet Earth

Earth is a planet. It is the planet where we live. Earth has land and water. It gets light and heat from the sun. Earth has one moon. Many people think there is life on other planets. Earth is the only planet that we know has life. Do you think there is life on other planets?

Unscramble.
Earth is the _planet_ where we live.
l e t p n a
2 5 6 1 4 3

Check.
☑ I have land and water.
☑ I get light and heat from the sun.
☐ I have five moons.
☑ I have one moon.
☑ I am a planet.

Circle.
Earth is the only planet that we know has ~~stars.~~ (life.)

Color.
Draw one yellow moon in the picture.

• Draw and color a picture of Earth.

Page 232

Man on the Moon

Do you ever look at the moon at night? The moon travels around the Earth. It gets its light from the sun. Men have gone to the moon in spaceships. They have walked on the moon. They even came back with moon rocks to study. Would you like to walk on the moon?

Circle.
The moon travels around the ~~room.~~ (Earth.)

Write.
The moon gets its light from the _sun_
Earth   sun

Check.
How did men go to the moon? ☑ spaceships
☐ automobiles

Circle.
Yes or No
Men have walked on the moon. (Yes) No

Circle.
What did men bring back from the moon? ~~stars~~ (rocks)

Color.
Draw a red spaceship on the moon.

• Draw what you would do if you went to the moon.

Page 233

A Falling Star

Have you ever seen a falling star? Falling stars are not really stars. They are small pieces of rock. As falling stars fall, they get hot and burn. They look big because they give off so much light. That is why they are so bright in the night sky. Did you know that meteor is another name for a falling star?

Circle.
Yes or No
A falling star is really a star.   Yes (No)
Falling stars are pieces of rock.   (Yes) No
Falling stars burn as they fall.   (Yes) No

Check.
Why does a falling star give off light?
☑ It gets hot and burns.
☐ It has a light bulb in it.

Unscramble.
Another name for a falling star is _meteor_
e r m o t e
2 6 1 5 3 4

Color.
Draw two yellow falling stars in the picture.

• Write a poem about a falling star.

Page 234

Far Out!

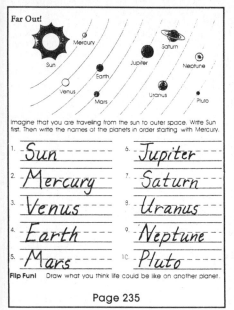

Imagine that you are traveling from the sun to outer space. Write Sun first. Then write the names of the planets in order starting with Mercury.

1. *Sun*   6. *Jupiter*
2. *Mercury*   7. *Saturn*
3. *Venus*   8. *Uranus*
4. *Earth*   9. *Neptune*
5. *Mars*   10. *Pluto*

Flip Fun! Draw what you think life could be like on another planet.

Page 235

Twinkling Starlights

Stars change as they get older. They start out big and then shrink. As they shrink, they change color. Color the stars the correct color.

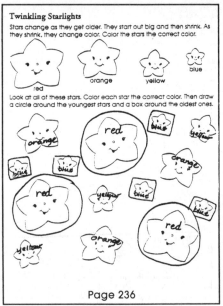

Look at all of these stars. Color each star the correct color. Then draw a circle around the youngest stars and a box around the oldest ones.

Page 236

Me, Myself, and I

1. Tell about yourself on the lines below.
2. Then draw a picture of yourself.

My name is _____

The color of my eyes is _____

The color of my hair is _____

This is me!

Page 237

I Am Special

1. Color the letters in the word [SPECIAL].
2. Cut and paste [SPECIAL] in the [ ] below.
3. Color the objects below.
4. Write a story telling why you are special.

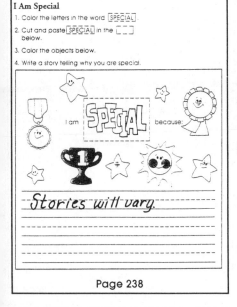

I am [SPECIAL] because:

Stories will vary.

Page 238

All About Me

Color and write.

Answers will vary.

My name _____

My school _____

My street _____

My phone _____

My city _____

My state _____

Page 239

Birthday Surprise!

1. Complete sentences 1 and 2.
2. Connect the numbers in the dot-to-dot.
3. Color 2 presents red and 3 presents blue.
4. Draw candles on the dot-to-dot picture to show how old you are.
5. Color the dot-to-dot.

1. My birthdate is _____ _____ _____
      month   date   year

2. I am _____ years old.

Page 240

Birthday Bonus Poster

Posters will vary.

My Cake   's Birthday   How I'll Look
                (date)

Where I'll Celebrate

Age I'll Be
(Make a big number and decorate it)

Friends I'll Invite
(Write their names and draw their pictures.)

My Gifts

My Birthday Dinner
(Draw what you'd like)

Page 241

Create a Cinquain — A Poem About Me

Line 1 = 1 word
Line 2 = 2 words describing line 1 (adjectives)
Line 3 = 3 action words (ending in ing)
Line 4 = a phrase expressing a feeling or observation about line 1
Line 5 = a word renaming or describing line 1

School
fun, exciting
learning, studying, playing
a great place to be
Elementary

Poems will vary.

Page 242

Feeling Fantastic!

People can have many feelings. They can be happy. They can be sad. Sometimes people can feel angry. Everyone has feelings.

People can have many (five) (feelings).

happy
angry
sad

sad
happy
angry

Make the faces look:

happy   sad   angry

• Draw and color a picture of how you feel.

Page 243

315   Daily Learning Drills Grade 1

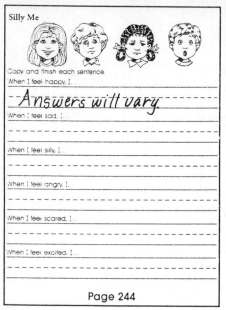

Silly Me

Copy and finish each sentence.

When I feel happy, I...

Answers will vary.

When I feel sad, I...

When I feel silly, I...

When I feel angry, I...

When I feel scared, I...

When I feel excited, I...

Page 244

My Family

1. Color the [house] roof brown.
2. Color the [chimney] chimney red.
3. Color the [bushes] bushes green.
4. Draw a picture of your family inside the house.
5. Write your address at the bottom of the page.

red

brown

green

My address is _____

Page 245

Family Puzzle

Draw family members, pets or fun things you do with your family over the entire puzzle. Color. Cut apart and give the whole puzzle to a classmate to put together.

Puzzles will vary.

Page 246

"My Mom"

Draw a picture of someone in your family.

Pictures and answers will vary.

Write one sentence to tell why this person is special.

Draw a picture of a gift you would like to give this person.

Page 247

Fun with Friends

A friend is someone you like very much. Friends play together. Friends help each other, too. It is nice to have many friends.

friend   from

A *friend* is someone you like.

Yes or No

Friends play together. (Yes) No
Friends are cars.   Yes (No)
Friends help each other. (Yes) No

Which are friends?

• Draw and color a picture of you and your friends.

Page 248

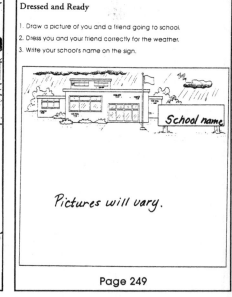

Dressed and Ready

1. Draw a picture of you and a friend going to school.
2. Dress you and your friend correctly for the weather.
3. Write your school's name on the sign.

School name

Pictures will vary.

Page 249

Special People

Use the code to name the special people below.

A	C	D	E	F	G	H		L	M	O	P	R	T
1	2	3	4	5	6	7	8	9	10	11	12	13	14

POLICE OFFICER

DOCTOR

FIRE FIGHTER

MAIL CARRIER

Page 250

What's My Job?

[Write] the correct word on each line. [Draw] a line to match the sentence.

pilot   farmer   doctor   builder   plumber   teacher

A *teacher* helps us learn new things.

A *pilot* flies planes many places.

A *farmer* plants and grows crops.

A *plumber* fixes many leaky pipes.

A *builder* builds new buildings.

A *doctor* helps people get well.

[Color] the pictures.

Page 251

My Teacher Helps Me Learn . . .

1. Circle the words from the Word Bank in the puzzle.
2. Then color the circled words green.
3. Last, write your teacher's name on the bottom line.

Word Bank
spelling science writing reading music
art math gym social studies

r	e	a	d	i	n	g	w	r	i	t	i	n	g
s	o	c	i	a	l	s	t	u	d	i	e	s	x
w	t	y	s	p	e	l	l	i	n	g	b	z	p
o	p	v	s	c	i	e	n	c	e	j	i	x	q
v	w	p	w	m	u	s	i	c	p	q	h	i	r
b	s	c	t	m	a	t	h	w	a	x	z	i	v
t	u	o	a	p	g	r	t	h	o	n	t	k	m
k	m	r	s	z	g	y	m	e	c	a	d	o	b	n

My teacher's name is _____

Page 252

Firefighter Find

A firefighter uses many things in his or her job.

Find the words from the Word Bank in the burning house below

Word Bank

boots	hat	oxygen mask	gloves
ax	hose	fire engine	ladder

Page 253

In the Cockpit

A pilot is a person who can fly an airplane. A pilot went to a special school to learn to fly a plane. Some pilots fly planes for fun. Some pilots fly planes as their jobs. A pilot sits in a special part of the plane called the cockpit. Have you ever seen a pilot sitting in the cockpit of a plane?

Write.
The person who flies an airplane is a _pilot_.
point   pilot

Circle.
Yes or No
A pilot went to a special school.   (Yes)   No
Some pilots fly just for fun.   (Yes)   No
A pilot drives a school bus.   Yes   (No)
Some pilots fly planes as their jobs.   (Yes)   No

Circle.
Where does a pilot sit to fly an airplane?
(cockpit)   bench   kitchen

Color.
Put green X's on the pilots.

• Draw a picture of a cockpit with you as the pilot.

Page 254

On the Farm

Farmers have a very important job. They grow most of the food that we eat. Some farmers grow plants such as oats, corn and wheat. Some farmers raise animals for food. They sell milk from cows. They sell eggs from chickens. Many farmers use machines to help them do their work.

Circle.
I grow (food) flowers for people to eat.
I raise trucks (animals) on my farm.

Check.
What plants do some farmers grow?
☑ oats
☑ corn
☐ steaks
☑ wheat

Match.
Which food comes from which animal?
milk ⟍ chickens
eggs ⟋ cows

Circle the words in the puzzle above.

• Draw a picture of three farm animals.

Page 255

We Care for You

Doctors help many people. They help sick people get well. They help healthy people stay well. People go to special schools to learn to be doctors. There are many kinds of doctors. There are doctors for children, eye doctors, ear doctors, bone doctors and heart doctors. Would you like to be a doctor?

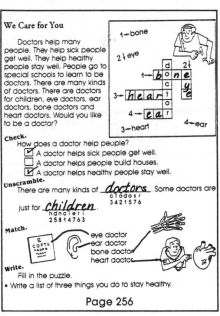

Check.
How does a doctor help people?
☑ A doctor helps sick people get well.
☐ A doctor helps people build houses.
☑ A doctor helps healthy people stay well.

Unscramble.
There are many kinds of _doctors_. Some doctors are
clodosr
3421576
just for _children_
hdncleri
25814763

Match.
eye doctor
ear doctor
bone doctor
heart doctor

Write.
Fill in the puzzle.
• Write a list of three things you do to stay healthy.

Page 256

Explorers of Space

An astronaut is a person who travels in space. Only a few people can become astronauts. They must be in very good health. They must be very smart. There are special schools to train astronauts. Some astronauts are scientists. Some are pilots. They must work hard to be ready to travel in space.

Unscramble.
A person who travels in space is an _astronaut_.
rtnotsaua
496532187

Check.
☐ Everyone can become an astronaut.
☑ An astronaut must be in very good health.
☑ An astronaut must be very smart.
☑ There are special schools to train astronauts.

Circle.
Some astronauts are: (scientists)   judges   (pilots)

Color.
Put a red circle around the space words.

• Draw a picture of where you would like to go in space.

Page 257

When I Grow Up . . .

Draw a line to the correct answer.

1. I want to help sick people.   policeman
2. I want to fly a plane.   teacher
3. I want to help people learn.   artist
4. I want to be in movies.   pilot
5. I want to keep people safe.   doctor
6. I want to help sick animals.   actor
7. I want to paint pretty pictures.   vet

Page 258

I Want to Be . . .

1. Draw a picture of what you might look like when you grow up.
2. Then write what you want to be when you are grown up and why.

When I grow up I want to be a _____

because _____

Answers will vary.

Page 259

Making a Map

1. Color and cut out the symbols.
2. Paste the symbols next to the matching words in the map key.
3. Then color the rest of the map.

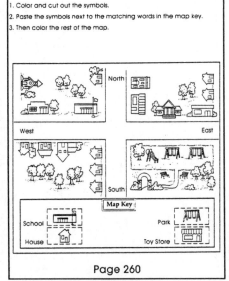

Page 260

A Venice Adventure

1. Start at the gondola, move 2 spaces south. Color the box blue.
2. Go east 2 spaces and draw a brown ⚓ anchor.
3. Go south 2 spaces and put an X in that box.
4. Move one space to the west and draw a red △ in that box.
5. Draw an oar in the second box south of the △.
6. Move 2 spaces east to get to the dock at the finish.

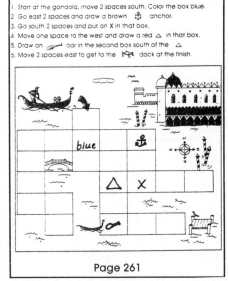

Page 261

Class Map

1. Add some symbols of your own to the map key.
2. Make a map of your classroom using the symbols found in the map key.
3. Add N, S, E, and W to your map.

Maps will vary.

W—|—E
N
S

Student's desk
Teacher's desk
Map Key

Page 262

Nick's Neighborhood

Draw a line along the path Nick used to get home.

1. Nick left the library and stopped to play on the school swings.
2. Next he looked at the puppies in the pet store window.
3. Nick watched as the fire truck raced out of the fire station.
4. Then Nick ran home to get money to buy an ice-cream cone.

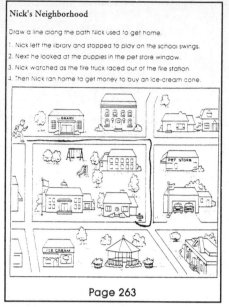

Page 263

Cities, Towns, and Rural Areas

1. Cut and paste the correct signs on each picture.
2. Draw a door on the barn.
3. Draw another tall building in the city.
4. Color the PARK sign yellow.
5. Write where you live in the last picture.
6. Color the pictures.

City Town

Answers will vary.

Rural Area

Page 264

Our State

1. Use a red crayon to outline your state.
2. Color the star yellow and the circle blue.
3. Cut and paste the star where the capital city is located.
4. Cut and paste the circle where your city is located.
5. Complete the sentences below.

This is our state.

Answers will vary.

The name of our state is _____
_____ is our capital city.
The city I live in, or near, is _____

Page 265

Our Country

1. Outline the map green.
2. Color your state blue. Mark an X where you live.
3. Color the rest of the map yellow.
4. Trace the sentence at the bottom in black.

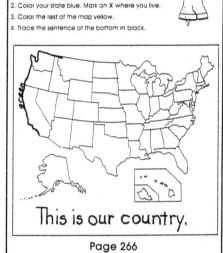

This is our country.

Page 266

Scrambled Continents

Unscramble the words below to spell the continents correctly. Remember to cross out the letters you use. Put in capitals where needed. Use the word bank to help you.

1. rtonh miecara — *North America*
2. cfIara — *Africa*
3. eropeu — *Europe*
4. uhots ecaamir — *South America*
5. saia — *Asia*
6. tnrtaiacac — *Antarctica*
7. asuriIaat — *Australia*

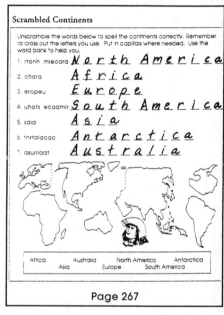

Africa   Australia   North America   Antarctica
Asia   Europe   South America

Page 267

Land Ho!

1. Draw a ◯ around the word mountains. Then color the mountains black.
2. Draw a ▢ around the word hills. Then color the hills green.
3. Draw a △ around the word plains. Then color the plains brown.
4. Put an X under the word water. Then color the water blue.

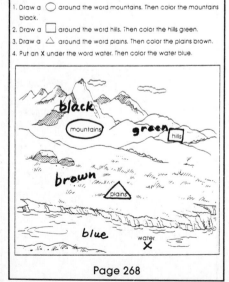

black — mountains
green — hills
brown — plains
blue — water X

Page 268

Home Rules

1. Number the pictures in the correct order.
2. Then color the pictures.

1 2 3

Keep your room clean.
Be helpful.
Take care of the yard.

Page 269

School Rules

1. Draw a red circle around the good rules.
2. Draw a black X on the bad rules.
3. Then write one of your school rules.

Run in the halls. ✗   Raise your hand in class.
Listen when your teacher talks.   Push friends when standing in line. ✗
Talk anytime in class. ✗   Walk in the halls.
Do not push friends when standing in line.   Fight with friends on the playground. ✗
Be noisy in the library. ✗   Be quiet in the library.
Quietly put school things away.   Stand up when riding the school bus. ✗
Throw paper on the floor. ✗   Clean up your lunch area.

One of our school rules is *Answers will vary.*

Page 270

Daily Learning Drills Grade 1

318

Traffic Signs and Signals

1. Color the STOP sign red.
2. Color the YIELD sign yellow.
3. DO NOT color the DO NOT ENTER sign.
4. Make the TRAFFIC LIGHT green.
5. Color the arrow on the ONE WAY sign black.
6. Color the WALK sign blue.

Page 271

Watch Out!

We should always obey safety rules.

1. Draw a black circle around five things that are wrong in the picture.
2. Then color the picture.

Page 272

Our State's Rules

1. Use the code to complete sentences 1, 2, and 3.
2. Then write your own answers for sentences 4 and 5.

A	C	E	G	I	L	N
1	3	5	7	9	12	14

O	P	R	S	T	V	W
15	16	19	19	20	22	23

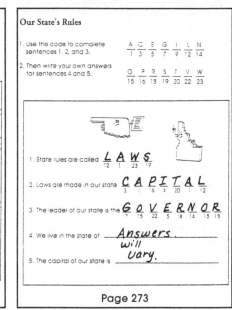

1. State rules are called **L A W S** 12 1 23 19
2. Laws are made in our state **C A P I T A L** 3 1 6 9 20 1 12
3. The leader of our state is the **G O V E R N O R** 7 15 22 5 18 14 15 18
4. We live in the state of ___Answers___
5. The capital of our state is ___will vary.___

Page 273

Our Nation's Laws

1. Use the Word Bank to write the answers for sentences 1, 2, and 3.
2. Write the name of our nation's President in sentence 4.
3. Draw a picture of our President inside the picture frame.
4. Color the frame and the picture.

Word Bank

President
laws
Washington, D.C.

1. Our nation's rules are called ___laws___
2. The White House is in ___Washington, D.C.___
3. Washington D.C. is where our ___President___ lives.
4. Our President's name is ___Answers will vary___

Page 274

Native American Tribes

1. Color the indian pictures and the different locations on the map.
2. Cut and paste the pictures correctly on the map.

This is where these Native Americans lived long ago.

Page 275

Native American Homes

1. Write teepee in box 1.
2. Write adobe in box 2.
3. Write wigwam in box 3.
4. Write longhouse in box 4.
5. Draw a sun on the teepee.
6. Color the longhouse brown.
7. Draw a door on the wigwam.
8. Draw small windows on the adobe.

1. teepee 2. adobe
3. wigwam 4. longhouse

Page 276

Native American Tools

1. Draw a red circle around the corn mortar and the salmon spear.
2. Draw a blue triangle around the digging stick and the fishhook.
3. Draw a green rectangle around the bow and arrow, the canoe paddle, and the hoe.
4. Draw a yellow square around the copper knife and the grinding stones.

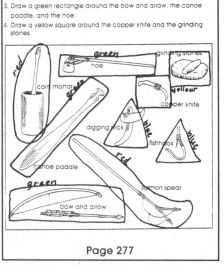

Page 277

The First Thanksgiving

Help the pilgrims find food for their first Thanksgiving.

1. Draw a brown circle around each type of food from the Word Bank hidden in the picture below.
2. Then color the picture.

Word Bank

corn	pumpkin
squash	turkey
onion	beans
berries	fish

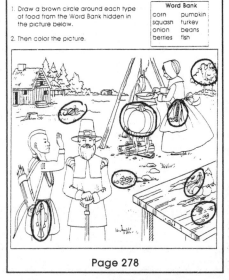

Page 278

A Whole New World

Write each word on the line next to the matching picture.

Word Bank

berries	corn	plant	indian	ocean
Pilgrim	ship	quail	forest	turkey

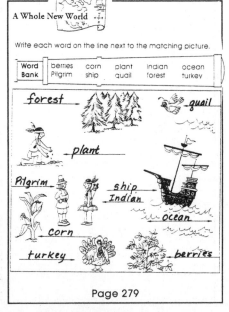

forest

quail

plant

Pilgrim

ship
Indian

corn

ocean

turkey

berries

Page 279

---

319   Daily Learning Drills Grade 1

Colonial Workers

1. Draw shoes in the window for the shoemaker.
2. Make some ⬭ dough for the baker to use to make bread.
3. Put a ⟼ hammer in the blacksmith's hand.
4. Draw a 👗 dress on the hanger for the dressmaker.
5. Draw a saddle for the saddlemaker.
6. Make sacks of ⬭ flour and ▯ sugar for the storekeeper.

Page 280

George Washington

1. Connect the dots beginning with number 1.
2. Color the dot-to-dot.
3. On the lines below write:
   George Washington was our first President.

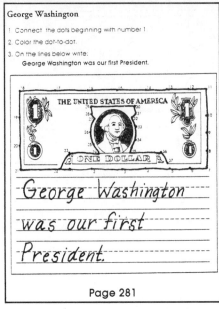

George Washington was our first President.

Page 281

Abraham Lincoln

1. Write the words from the Word Bank under the correct pictures.
2. Then color the pictures.

Word Bank
log cabin
string tie
top hat
White House
ax
books

Abraham Lincoln as a boy — *log cabin, ax, books*
Abraham Lincoln as President — *string tie, top hat, White House*

Page 282

Clara Barton

1. Color the medicine bottle brown.
2. Draw a bandage on the man's leg.
3. Color the cross on the wagon red.
4. Color Clara Barton's bag black.
5. Now color the rest of the picture.

Page 283

Martin Luther King, Jr.

1. Color the W's black.
2. Color the X's blue.
3. Color the Y's brown
4. Color the Z's pink.
5. Color the V's green.

Page 284

Sally Ride

1. Color only the things Sally Ride would need in space.
2. Cut out and paste the colored pictures in the boxes below.
3. Then color Sally Ride.

First Woman in Space – June 1983

Page 285

Person I Most Admire

1. Think about the person you most admire.
2. Complete the sentences below.
3. Then draw a picture of yourself with that person.

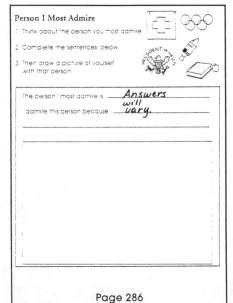

The person I most admire is _Answers_
I admire this person because _will vary._

Page 286

An African Aunt

1. Read each sentence and write the letter on the ant.
2. Then write each letter in order to find the answer to the riddle at the bottom.

1. Find the ninth letter in crocodile. **e**
2. Write the first letter in lion. **l**
3. What is the last letter in giraffe? **e**
4. Find the middle letter in ape. **p**
5. What letter is at the end of cheetah? **h**
6. Write the fifth letter in zebra. **a**
7. Find the last letter in python. **n**
8. Write the third letter in ostrich. **t**

What animal has the biggest aunt?
An **e l e p h a n t**

Page 287

Chinese Challenge

Use the Word Bank to write the correct words in the sentences.

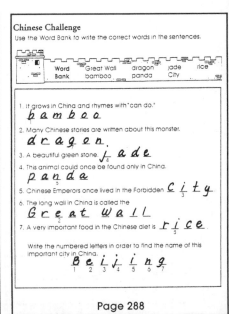

Word Bank Great Wall   dragon   jade   rice
bamboo   panda   City

1. It grows in China and rhymes with "can do."
   b a m b o o
2. Many Chinese stories are written about this monster.
   d r a g o n.
3. A beautiful green stone. **J a d e**
4. This animal could once be found only in China.
   p a n d a
5. Chinese Emperors once lived in the Forbidden **C i t y**
6. The long wall in China is called the
   G r e a t   W a l l
7. A very important food in the Chinese diet is **r i c e**

Write the numbered letters in order to find the name of this important city in China.
B e i j i n g
  1   2   3   4   5   6   7

Page 288

Name _____

ABC Planets

Write the names of the planets in ABC order.

1. _____

2. _____

3. _____

4. _____

5. _____

6. _____

7. _____

8. _____

9. _____

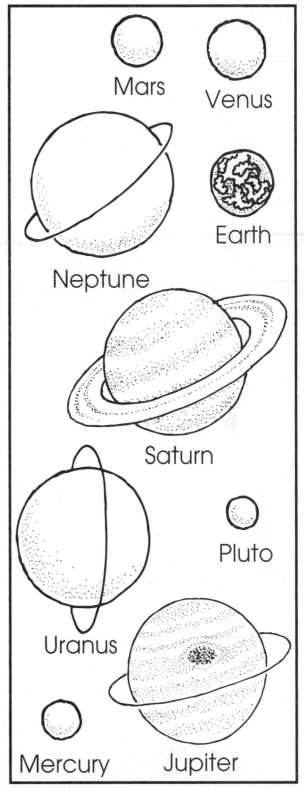

Mars   Venus

Earth

Neptune

Saturn

Pluto

Uranus   Jupiter

Mercury

Name _____

3-2-1 Blastoff!

Find and circle 9 hidden pictures that begin with **b**.

 book   bell   bat

 bus   bib   bow

ball   bone   bun

Name _____

An Icy Path

Help the penguins get to the iceberg. Say the name of each picture on the path. Circle the beginning sound.

Daily Learning Drills Grade 1

Name _____

Up, Up, and Away!

Look at the pictures behind each plane.
Color the pictures that begin with the sound
of the letter on the plane.

Name _____

Hooray for Consonants!

Say the name of each picture. Write the letter that makes the beginning sound.

_____

_____

_____

_____

_____

_____

_____

_____

_____

_____

_____

_____

_____

_____

_____

Name _____

Animals, Animals

Say the name of each animal. Circle the letter that makes the ending sound. Then color the pictures.

t   z   g   b   n   l   v   x

z   g   b   t   s   b   g   m

w   n   l   k   r   d   p   h

Name _____

Plucky's Pictures

Plucky Duck drew pictures of things that have a short **u** sound. Look at the pictures below. Which ones did Plucky draw? Color them.

Daily Learning Drills Grade 1

Name _____

Rainy Day Puddles

Look at the pictures on the umbrellas. Write their names on the puddles. Use the words on the rain cloud.

cup   sun   jug   rug
bus   nut   bug   duck

Name _____

What's Hiding?

Find out what is hiding below. If a space has a picture of a short o word, color it red. Color the other spaces yellow.

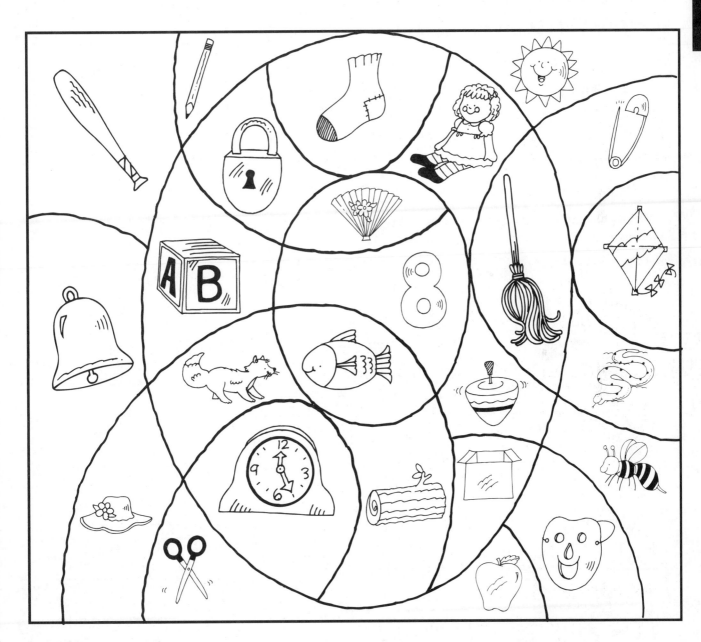

What was hiding? _____

Daily Learning Drills Grade 1

Name _____

Hunt for Short O

Dottie Fox looked in her home for things that have short **o** in their names. Read the list she made. Write each word under the matching picture.

pot   top
mop   doll
box   sock
lock   clock

_____

- - - - - - - - - - -

_____

_____

- - - - - - - - - - -

_____

_____

- - - - - - - - - - -

_____

_____

- - - - - - - - - - -

_____

_____

- - - - - - - - - - -

_____

_____

- - - - - - - - - - -

_____

_____

- - - - - - - - - - -

_____

_____

- - - - - - - - - - -

_____

Name _____

Name the Pictures
Label the pictures below.
Use the words in the box.

cake	gate	tape
rake	vase	cane
cape	cave	game

_____

- - - - - - - - - - - - - - - -

_____

_____

- - - - - - - - - - - - - - - -

_____

_____

- - - - - - - - - - - - - - - -

_____

_____

- - - - - - - - - - - - - - - -

_____

_____

- - - - - - - - - - - - - - - -

_____

_____

- - - - - - - - - - - - - - - -

_____

_____

- - - - - - - - - - - - - - - -

_____

_____

- - - - - - - - - - - - - - - -

_____

_____

- - - - - - - - - - - - - - - -

_____

Daily Learning Drills Grade 1

Name _____

What Will They Do?

Look at the picture clues. Write the correct word for each sentence.

1. Dale will bake a _____ .
   cake   cane

2. Jane will swim in the _____ .
   late   lake

3. Nate will play a _____ .
   game   gate

4. Dave will help Dad _____ .
   rate   rake

5. Kate will wash the _____ .
   plate   place

6. Jake will _____ at the rink.
   skate   snake

Name _____

Let's Read Long e Words!

Look at each picture.
Write the long **e** word.

Long e Words	
bead	read
dream	seal
leaf	wheat
peach	

Daily Learning Drills Grade 1

Name _____

Hidden Picture Fun

Can you find **9** hidden pictures of long **i** words? Circle them.

 bike

 five

 hive

 kite

 lime

 dime

 nine

 pipe

 slide

Name _____

Let's Sail

Write the answer to each riddle.
Use the long **a** words in the box.

mail	nail	pail
sail	tail	wail

1. This is part of a boat.

_____

- -

_____

2. A dog wags this.

_____

- -

_____

3. It carries water.

_____

- -

_____

4. You hit this with a hammer.

_____

- -

_____

5. You can read this.

_____

- -

6. This means "to cry."

_____

- -

Name _____

A Cute Mule

Circle the long **u** word that matches each picture.

cute	tube
rule	dune
mule	dude
prune	glue
Sue	fume
cube	June
blue	flute
tune	rude

Name _____

Rhyme Time Fun

Look at the pictures.
Write a sentence that tells about each picture.
Hint: Each sentence will have two rhyming long **o** words.

toad

road

boat

moat

coat

goat

A _____ is in the moat.

The _____ is wearing a _____.

A _____ is on the _____.

Daily Learning Drills Grade 1

Name _____

Words and Meanings

Read the two words on each dinosaur.
If they have the same meaning, color the dinosaur **green**.
If they do not have the same meaning, color the dinosaur **red**.

Name _____

Compound It

Draw lines between pairs of words to make compound words. Then write the words.

pine   corn   _____

bird   apple   _____

hot   ball   _____

pop   dog   _____

foot   house   _____

Name _____

Space Questions

Questions often begin
with these words.

Who
What
When
Where
Why

Complete each sentence with the correct word from the box

1. _____ can become an astronaut?

2. _____ do people want to be astronauts?

3. _____ is the space shuttle kept?

4. _____ will there be a shuttle launch?

5. _____ do astronauts wear in space?

Name _____

On the Moon

Circle the sentences that tell about the picture.
Write them on the lines. Read the story.

They are on the moon.   There are tall green trees.

The flag is flying.   One astronaut is driving.

_____

- -

_____

- -

_____

- -

_____

- -

Name _____

Gentle Giraffes

Color the circles.
Then color the rest of the picture.

Name _____

Roarin' Rhino

Color the triangles. Then color the rest of the picture.

Daily Learning Drills Grade 1

Name _____

Polar Bear Palace

Circle the **6** mistakes in the picture. Color.

Name _____

Perfect Peacocks

Count the number of feathers on each peacock.
Write the number on the line.

Name _____

Hum a Sweet Tune

Connect the dots from **1** to **20**. Color.

Name _____

Fill It In

Write in the missing numbers.

1			4					9	
	12					17			
		23					28		
31				35					
	42								
			54						
	62					67			
		73							
					86				
				95					

Name _____

Even More Fun!

Find the even number words hidden in the puzzle. Words go across, down, and diagonally. Use the Word Bank to help you.

Word Bank

two	twelve
four	fourteen
six	sixteen
eight	eighteen
ten	

a	b	t	f	b	d	i	j	a	q	a	r	a
w	f	e	w	e	f	o	u	r	t	e	e	n
c	o	d	i	e	h	a	z	p	d	s	b	w
v	u	g	u	g	l	s	i	x	t	e	e	n
c	r	t	k	m	h	v	o	z	i	w	i	h
l	x	e	i	g	h	t	e	e	n	t	o	y
d	e	n	y	m	e	y	n	s	i	x	o	p

Name _____

Garden Friends

Circle the animal that comes next in each row.

Daily Learning Drills Grade 1

Name _____

What Comes Next?
Complete each pattern by drawing a picture in the blank.

1.

2.

3.

4.

Name _____

Blast Off!

Count by 2's to complete the picture and find out where your imagination can take you! Then color the picture.

Daily Learning Drills Grade 1

Name _____

Rockin' Roller Coaster

Write numbers on the cars, counting by 5's.

Name _____

Swift Swimmers

Add. Color the spaces on the fish that match each sum as you go. The fish to be completely covered is the fastest swimmer.

$$
\begin{array}{r} 5 \\ + 3 \\ \hline \end{array}
\qquad
\begin{array}{r} 7 \\ + 5 \\ \hline \end{array}
\qquad
\begin{array}{r} 2 \\ + 0 \\ \hline \end{array}
\qquad
\begin{array}{r} 6 \\ + 4 \\ \hline \end{array}
\qquad
\begin{array}{r} 3 \\ + 2 \\ \hline \end{array}
$$

$$
\begin{array}{r} 6 \\ + 5 \\ \hline \end{array}
\qquad
\begin{array}{r} 5 \\ + 2 \\ \hline \end{array}
\qquad
\begin{array}{r} 6 \\ + 3 \\ \hline \end{array}
\qquad
\begin{array}{r} 3 \\ + 3 \\ \hline \end{array}
\qquad
\begin{array}{r} 3 \\ + 1 \\ \hline \end{array}
$$

Daily Learning Drills Grade I

Name _____

What's the Scoop?

Add.

12 + 3	11 + 12	54 + 32	71 + 28	96 + 3	70 + 18
55 + 33	16 + 82	35 + 64	17 + 42	81 + 17	13 + 15
64 + 24	78 + 11	22 + 65	14 + 33	40 + 50	60 + 15
18 + 41	44 + 22	15 + 44	49 + 30	19 + 50	43 + 16

Name _____

Weather Report: Snowy

Subtract. Connect the dots in order from least to greatest to find the hidden picture.

Start 5 – 5 = ☐

Start •

4 – 3 = ☐

4 – 3 = ☐

6 – 4 = ☐   •   5 – 3 = ☐

5 – 2 = ☐ •   • 7 – 4 = ☐

7 – 3 = ☐ •   • 8 – 4 = ☐

• 6 – 1 = ☐

8 – 3 = ☐ •

7 – 1 = ☐ •   • 8 – 2 = ☐

MATH REVIEW

Name _____

Weather Chart

Use information from the graph to find the answers.

This Month's Weather

rainy	⦸⦸	|||| ||
cloudy ☁	|||| ||
sunny ☀	|||| |||
windy 🍃	|||
snowy ❄	||||

How many more days were ⦸⦸ than 🍃 ? _____ - _____ = _____	How many more days were ☁ than ❄ ? _____ - _____ = _____
How many more days were ☀ than 🍃 ? _____ - _____ = _____	How many more days were ❄ than 🍃 ? _____ - _____ = _____
How many more days were ☀ than ☁ ? _____ - _____ = _____	How many more days were ☀ than ⦸⦸ ? _____ - _____ = _____

Name _____

Be a Super Solver

1. Mary saw 4 chickens by the barn. Then she saw 3 more hiding by the gate. How many chickens did Mary see? Show your work.

_____ chickens

2. John had 8 cookies. He gave 5 to his sister. How many cookies did John have left? Show your work.

_____ cookies

3. Jim and Pam have 8 balls in all. Jim has 2 more than Pam.

How many balls does Jim have? _____

How many balls does Pam have? _____

Show your work.

Name _____

Half For You, Half For Me

When you divide something in half, you divide it into two equal parts. For example, if you had two candy bars and you gave one to your friend, you would have given him or her one-half of what you had.

Color one-half of the items in each group below.

1.

2.

3.

4.

5.

6.

Name _____

Use Good Cents

Count the money. Write each amount.

A.   _____ ¢

B.   _____ ¢

C.   _____ ¢

D.   _____ ¢

E.   _____ ¢

F.   _____ ¢

MATH REVIEW

Name _____

Circle Up

Circle the coins to show each amount.

35¢	20¢
14¢	43¢
25¢	54¢
30¢	47¢

Name _____

Time Flies

Draw hands on the clocks.

12:00

4:30

8:00

5:30

7:00

6:30

3:00

9:30

Daily Learning Drills Grade 1

Name _____

Bar Graph Fun

Fill in the bar graph for the correct number of toys in each category.

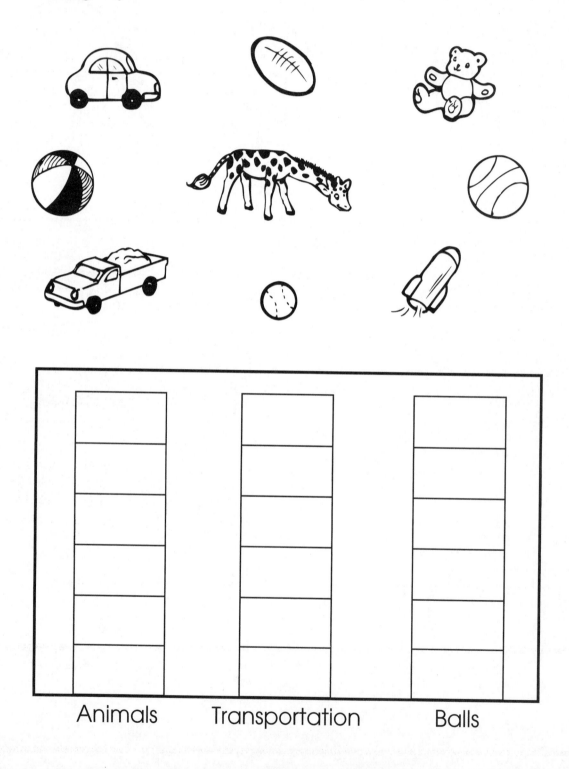

Name _____

An Inch Is an Inch

Cut the ruler from the bottom of the page. Measure each object to the nearest inch. Write the number of inches on each line.

A. _____

B. _____

C. _____

D. _____

Daily Learning Drills Grade 1

Name _____

Plants

Plants need water, sun, soil, and air to grow.
Some plants have flowers. Plants grow from seeds. Some
parts of a plant are the stem, the roots, and the leaves.
Color the picture.

Daily Learning Drills Grade I

Name _____

Plants (continued)

Answer the questions.

1. What do plants need to grow?

_____

_____

_____

_____

2. What do plants grow from?

_____

_____

_____

3. What are some plant parts?

_____

_____

_____

_____

_____

_____

Name _____

How Does Your Garden Grow?

Color the pictures. Then cut out the pictures and use them in a garden mobile. Tape each oval to a string.

Daily Learning Drills Grade 1

SCIENCE REVIEW

Name _____

What's in the Garden?

Color these things found in a garden.
Use the number key to help you.

7 = green   **8** = red   **9** = orange

SCIENCE REVIEW

Name _____

Letter Mix-Up

Help! The farm animals' names are all mixed up.
Help Dana spell them correctly on the line
beside each "mixed-up" word.

1. wco : _____

2. sehor : _____   7. nhe : _____

3. eepsh : _____   8. ckdu : _____

4. oatg : _____   9. keyrut : _____

5. tac : _____   10. gdo : _____

6. terroos : _____   11. gpi : _____

Name _____

You Decide

Circle yes or no.

1. Does a dog have two ears?   yes   no

2. Can a frog push a truck?   yes   no

3. Will a fox eat a bird?   yes   no

4. Do pigs have wings?   yes   no

5. Will a seal eat a fish?   yes   no

6. Can a turtle fly?   yes   no

7. Can a seal swim?   yes   no

8. Can a cat read?   yes   no

9. Do giraffes have long necks?   yes   no

Daily Learning Drills Grade 1

Name _____

What Belongs at the Zoo?

Color the animals.

Draw a **red** circle around the animals that live at home.

Draw a **blue** square around the animals that live at the zoo.

Name _____

Step into the Wild

Write the name of each zoo animal.
Use the Word Bank to help.

1.

2.

3.

4.

5. _____

6.

_____

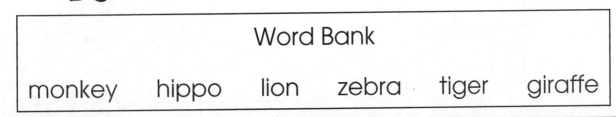

Word Bank
monkey   hippo   lion   zebra   tiger   giraffe

Daily Learning Drills Grade 1

Name _____

A Snake Story

Read the story, then draw the pictures following the directions. After you read the story, answer the questions.

Tim did not want to go to the zoo. His big sister Kate was teasing him. "Tim is a scaredy-cat. Tim is a scaredy-cat!"

"I am not!" said Tim. But Tim really was afraid. He was afraid of one kind of animal at the zoo—the snakes.

Tim's dad told him that the snakes were in glass cages and couldn't get out. But that didn't matter to Tim. He didn't even like to look at them.

At the zoo, Tim, Kate, and their dad saw elephants, zebras, alligators, and monkeys. They ate candy and popcorn. Then, Tim saw the scary sign! It said, "SNAKES"!

(Draw the snake sign.)

Name _____

Kate walked to the cages. Tim's dad held his hand. "You decide, son," his dad said. Tim took a deep breath and said, "Let's go."

A zookeeper was cleaning the snake cages. Kate got as close to the glass as she could. Tim stood back by the wall.

"Are those snakes slimy?" Kate asked the zookeeper.

"No, they're not," the zookeeper replied. "They feel like your skin. But they have scales, so they feel a bit bumpier."

"What do they eat?" asked Kate as Tim stepped closer.

"They eat live mice," the zookeeper answered.

"Will they hurt me?" asked Tim as he took one last step and placed his face next to the glass cage.

(Draw a picture of Tim looking at the snakes.)

Name _____

A Snake Story (continued)

The zookeeper said, "Well, these snakes are safely locked behind the glass. Snakes don't want to hurt anybody. They're just trying to survive. But sometimes people scare them, so they try to defend themselves. That's when people can get hurt."

The zookeeper left, and Tim, Kate, and their dad stared into the cage. The snakes stared back.

"I guess you're not scared anymore, Tim," said Kate.

"Well, once you learn about something, it's not as scary. Besides, they are behind glass!" replied Tim. They all laughed together.

Answer "T" for true or "F" for false.

1. Snakes eat popcorn. _____

2. Snakes are slimy. _____

3. Snakes might hurt you when trying to defend themselves. _____

4. Tim ran away from the snakes. _____

5. After Tim learned about the snakes, he wasn't afraid anymore. _____

Name _____

A Ladybug Story

Read the story. Then answer the questions that follow.

Ladybugs are insects. Ladybugs hatch from eggs. As they grow, they change in color from pale orange to red with black spots. Ladybugs eat aphids. Aphids are little green bugs that live on roses and other plants. Ladybugs can fly because they have wings. The red part of a ladybug's body is called the "wing case." They do not fly very fast. Ladybugs sleep through the winter under piles of leaves. In the spring, ladybugs wake up. Time to get busy, ladybugs!

1. What are ladybugs? _____

2. What do ladybugs eat? _____

3. What are aphids? _____

4. What is the red part of a ladybug's body called?

_____

5. What do ladybugs do during the winter? _____

Name _____

For the Birds

Winter, spring, summer, fall,

all the robins do is call,

for spring, summer, fall, winter,

huddled in their nests a-twitter.

Summer, fall, winter, spring,

can't help themselves, they must sing,

through fall, winter, spring, summer,

teaching me to be a hummer.

Hum, hum, hum, hum, hum, hum, hum!

Hum, hum, hum, hum, hum, hum, hum!

Color each picture, then write the season underneath.

_____

_____

_____

_____

Name _____

Graph It!

Complete the graph below by asking six people what their favorite season is. Color a square for each response. Start coloring squares at the bottom of the graph first.
Then answer the questions below.

What Is Your Favorite Season?

Number of People

	Winter	Spring	Summer	Fall

1. Which season did most of the people like? _____

2. Which season did the fewest people like? _____

3. What did you learn from this graph? _____

_____

4. What can't you learn from this graph? _____

_____

SCIENCE REVIEW

Name _____

Into Outer Space

Finish the sentence.
Draw a picture of a spaceship.

One planet I want to

visit is

Here is a picture of the spaceship I would like to take to go there.

Name _____

Found in Space

Read each riddle. Write the answer.

float
stars
Mars
sun
Earth
craters
shuttle
Saturn

1. This huge star lights the day. ___ ___ ___

2. These shine at night. ___ ___ ___ ___ ___

3. These are on the moon. ___ ___ ___ ___ ___ ___ ___

4. This is our home planet. ___ ___ ___ ___ ___

5. This flies into space. ___ ___ ___ ___ ___ ___ ___

6. This planet is red. ___ ___ ___ ___

7. This planet has rings. ___ ___ ___ ___ ___ ___

8. Astronauts do this in space. ___ ___ ___ ___ ___

SCIENCE REVIEW

Name _____

The Space Shuttle
Read the story.

The space shuttle takes astronauts into space. Rockets launch the shuttle. The shuttle orbits the earth. The astronauts do work in space. They may set up satellites or do experiments. When it is time to return, the shuttle lands on a runway. The astronauts are back on earth.

Answer the questions.

1. What takes astronauts into space? _____

_____

2. What launches the shuttle into space? _____

_____

3. What kind of work do astronauts do in space? _____

_____

4. Where does the shuttle land when it returns to earth?

_____

Name _____

Fossil Find

Draw a line to match the fossil imprint with the object that made it.

Name _____

Dinosaur Giants

The biggest dinosaurs were plant-eaters. They had heavy legs and big bodies. Their heads were small but their necks were long.

These huge dinosaurs had to eat a lot of food. They may have walked very far to find all the food they needed.

They used their long necks to eat food at the tops of trees. They may have even stood on their hind legs to get food.

Can you find these words in the puzzle? Circle each one.

☐ huge

☐ body

☐ head

☐ neck

☐ food

☐ walk

☐ eat

☐ legs

b	r	l	e	g	s	r
o	m	h	r	w	p	d
d	z	u	l	a	m	h
y	o	g	d	l	e	e
a	n	e	c	k	v	a
e	a	t	f	o	o	d

Name _____

Dinosaur Riddles

Read each riddle.
Draw a line to the matching picture.

I had a big head.
I had long, sharp teeth.
Who was I?

Diplodocus

I had a big head.
I had three sharp horns.
Who was I?

Parasaurolophus

I had a small head.
I had a long, long neck.
Who was I?

Tyrannosaurus

I had a mouth like a duck.
I had a long crest.
Who was I?

Triceratops

SCIENCE REVIEW

Name _____

Write a Letter!

Write a letter to your best friend. Tell him or her about what you did last summer. Ask your friend some questions about what he or she has been doing. Ask your parents to help you mail the letter.

_____
(today's date)

Dear _____,

_____

_____

_____

_____

_____

_____

From,

_____
(your name)

Name _____

Make a List

You are having a party. List the people you want to invite. Then list the food you will have at the party.

Guests	Food
1.	1.
2.	2.
3.	3.
4.	4.
5.	5.

Daily Learning Drills Grade 1

SOCIAL STUDIES REVIEW

Name _____

Dining Manners

Help Polite Pig teach his friends some table manners. Write the missing word to begin each rule. Draw a line from the rule to the friend who needs to learn it.

___ ___ ___ ___ with your mouth closed.

___ ___ ___ a spoon or fork to eat most foods.

___ ___ ___ your food into bite-size pieces.

___ ___ ___ your napkin on your lap to begin.

Name _____

What Is Happening?

Circle the names of things in the picture.

fossils	tools	dog
snowman	workers	camera
dirt	hat	money

Circle and write the best title for the picture.

Hiking in the Desert   Finding Fossils   At the Museum

_____

- -

_____

SOCIAL STUDIES REVIEW

Name _____

Community Workers

Read each riddle.
Draw a line to the matching picture.

I come to your house.
I bring something.
It has a stamp.
Who am I?

life guard

I work in a store.
I help you find things.
I take your money.
Who am I?

baker

I work at the pool.
I am a good swimmer.
I can save lives.
Who am I?

mail carrier

I start early each day.
I mix up some dough.
Then I bake it.
Who am I?

sales clerk

Name _____

Where Do They Work?

Cut out the community workers.
Paste them on the map at the places where they work.

Daily Learning Drills Grade 1

SOCIAL STUDIES REVIEW

Name _____

Getting There

The children are walking through the town square to the bus stop. Draw a line to show the path they will take.

Name _____

My Community

Finish the sentences. Draw a picture to match.

The name of my community

is

One place I like to visit is

Here is a picture of the place.

Name _____

About My Community

Write about your community.

I live in

_____
- -
_____ .

It is in the state of

_____
- -
_____ .

I live in or near a

_____
- -
_____ .

| suburb   city   farm   town |

This is a picture that shows me shopping at the market.

In winter the weather is

_____
- -
_____ .

In summer the weather is

_____
- -
_____ .

My community is in or near

☐ mountains.
☐ a desert.
☐ a plain.
☐ a valley.
☐ hills.

The water nearest my community is

☐ an ocean.
☐ a river.
☐ a lake.
☐ a swamp.

Daily Learning Drills Grade 1

Name _____

A Busy Community

People live, work, and play together in a community.
Look at each picture. Circle the sentence that matches it.

They will ride their bikes.

They will ride the bus.

They are going shopping.

They are going to the park.

Someone needs help.

Someone is late.

The library is open.

The library is closed.

The firefighters are playing.

The firefighters are working.

It is a school day.

It is a weekend day.

Name _____

Recycle It!

These pictures show a busy day at a recycling center.
Can you find **10** differences between the two pictures?

What does your family or your community recycle?

_____

....

_____

SOCIAL STUDIES REVIEW

Name _____

Community Center

Have you ever been to a community center? At a community center, you can do many fun things.

You can take an art class or learn how to swim. There might be a gym where people can exercise.

At some community centers there is a special wall. Kids can learn to rock climb on the wall!

Can you find these words in the puzzle?
Circle each one.

☐ center   ☐ class

☐ learn   ☐ swim

☐ gym   ☐ climb

☐ wall   ☐ fun

w	q	u	l	e	x	c
a	g	y	m	f	c	e
l	r	m	a	u	l	n
l	e	a	r	n	i	t
c	a	s	w	i	m	e
c	l	a	s	s	b	r

Name _____

In the Mountains

Read the story.

Have you ever been to a mountain community? Most mountain communities are far from busy cities. Some people live in the mountains all year. Other people visit the mountains on vacation. In the winter, they ski or play in the snow. In the summer they might rest, hike, and ride bikes.

Finish the sentences.

1. Most mountain communities are _____ from busy cities.

2. Some people live in the mountains all _____ .

3. In the _____, people like to ski.

4. In the summer, they might ride _____ .

Name _____

Good Citizens

Write the word that completes each sentence.

1. Good citizens obey the _____ .

| laws |
| cats |

2. They _____ their communities.

| ride |
| help |

3. Good citizens care for _____ .

| happy |
| earth |

4. They try to be good _____ .

| neighbors |
| shoes |

5. They vote for their _____ .

| floor |
| leaders |

6. You can be a good _____ .

| car |
| citizen |

Name _____

Some Super Signs

Look at each sign. Read the questions. Circle the correct answers.

A.

B.

C.

D.

1. Which sign tells you not to walk there?

    Sign A   Sign D   Sign B

2. Which sign tells you that something is for sale?

    Sign C   Sign B   Sign A

3. Which sign tells you which way to the pool?

    Sign B   Sign C   Sign A

4. Which sign tells you how to get out?

    Sign C   Sign B   Sign D

SOCIAL S

Name _____

Map Activity

Follow the directions to color the map of Kenya.

1. Draw a wooden sailboat in the Indian Ocean.
2. Color the Great Rift Valley brown.
   Draw a blue star where Nairobi is marked.
   Color the dome-shaped hut red.
   or Lake Turkana and Lake Victoria blue.

Name _____

African Life

Color and cut out these pictures of African life. Divide the pictures into two piles, one for traditional items and the other for modern items.

Review Answer Key

Daily Learning Drills Grade

Hunt for Short O

Dottie Fox looked in her home for things that have short **o** in their names. Read the list she made. Write each word under the matching picture.

pot	top
mop	doll
box	sock
lock	clock

top   pot

clock   lock   mop

box   doll   sock

330

Name the Pictures

Label the pictures below. Use the words in the box.

cake	gate	tape
rake	vase	cane
cape	cave	game

rake   cave   tape

gate   vase   game

cake   cape   cane

331

What Will They Do?

Look at the picture clues. Write the correct word for each sentence.

1. Dale will bake a **cake** .
   cake   cane

2. Jane will swim in the **lake** .
   late   lake

3. Nate will play a **game** .
   game   gate

4. Dave will help Dad **rake** .
   rate   rake

5. Kate will wash the **plate** .
   plate   place

6. Jake will **skate** at the rink.
   skate   snake

332

Let's Read Long "e" Words!

Look at each picture. Write the long **e** word.

Long e Words	
bead	read
dream	seal
leaf	wheat
peach	

l e a f

r e a d   d r e a m

s e a l   p e a c h

b e a d   w h e a t

333

Hidden Picture Fun

Can you find **9** hidden pictures of **long i** words? Circle them.

bike   kite   nine
five   lime   pipe
hive   dime   slide

334

Let's Sail

Write the answer to each riddle. Use the long **a** words in the box.

mail	nail	pail
sail	tail	wail

1. This is part of a boat.
   sail

2. A dog wags this.
   tail

3. It carries water.
   pail

4. You hit this with a hammer.
   nail

5. You can read this.
   mail

6. This means "to cry."
   wail

335

A Cute Mule

Circle the long **u** word that matches each picture.

cute / rule	tube / dune
mule / prune	dude / glue
Sue / cube	fume / June
blue / tune	flute / rude

336

Rhyme Time Fun

Look at the pictures. Write a sentence that tells about each picture.
Hint: Each sentence will have two rhyming long **o** words.

toad
boat
road
coat
goat
moat

A **boat** is in the moat .

The **goat** is wearing a **coat** .

A **toad** is on the **road** .

337

Words and Meanings

Read the two words on each dinosaur. If they have the same meaning, color the dinosaur **green**. If they do not have the same meaning, color the dinosaur **red**.

green   green
red
green
green
green
red   green

338

Compound It
Draw lines between pairs of words to make compound words. Then write the words.

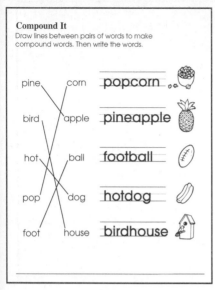

pine   corn   popcorn

bird   apple   pineapple

hot   ball   football

pop   dog   hotdog

foot   house   birdhouse

339

Space Questions
Questions often begin with these words.

Who
What
When
Where
Why

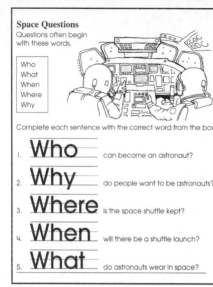

Complete each sentence with the correct word from the box.

1. **Who** can become an astronaut?

2. **Why** do people want to be astronauts?

3. **Where** is the space shuttle kept?

4. **When** will there be a shuttle launch?

5. **What** do astronauts wear in space?

340

On the Moon
Circle the sentences that tell about the picture. Write them on the lines. Read the story.

They are on the moon.   There are tall green trees.
The flag is flying.   One astronaut is driving.

341

Gentle Giraffes
Color the circles.
Then color the rest of the picture.

342

Roarin' Rhino
Color the triangles. Then color the rest of the picture.

Rhinoceros

343

Polar Bear Palace
Circle the 6 mistakes in the picture. Color.

344

Perfect Peacocks
Count the number of feathers on each peacock.
Write the number on the line.

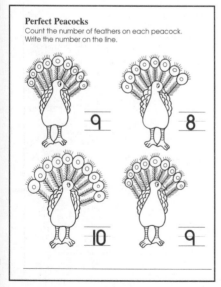

9   8

10   9

345

Hum a Sweet Tune
Connect the dots from 1 to 20. Color.

346

Fill It In
Write in the missing numbers.

1	2	3	4	5	6	7	8	9	10
11	12	13	14	15	16	17	18	19	20
21	22	23	24	25	26	27	28	29	30
31	32	33	34	35	36	37	38	39	40
41	42	43	44	45	46	47	48	49	50
51	52	53	54	55	56	57	58	59	60
61	62	63	64	65	66	67	68	69	70
71	72	73	74	75	76	77	78	79	80
81	82	83	84	85	86	87	88	89	90
91	92	93	94	95	96	97	98	99	100

347

Even More Fun!
Find the even number words hidden in the puzzle. Words go across, down, and diagonally. Use the Word Bank to help you.

Word Bank

two	twelve
four	fourteen
six	sixteen
eight	eighteen
ten	

348

Garden Friends
Circle the animal that comes next in each row.

349

What Comes Next?
Complete each pattern by drawing a picture in the blank.

1.

2.

3.

4.

350

Blast Off!
Count by 2s to complete the picture and find out where your imagination can take you! Then color the picture.

351

Rockin' Roller Coaster
Write numbers on the cars, counting by 5s.

352

Swift Swimmers
Add. Color the spaces on the fish that match each sum as you go. The fish to be completely covered is the fastest swimmer.

5 + 3 8	7 + 5 12	2 + 0 2	6 + 4 10	3 + 2 5
6 + 5 11	5 + 2 7	6 + 3 9	3 + 3 6	3 + 1 4

353

What's the Scoop?
Add.

12 + 3 15	11 + 12 23	54 + 32 86	71 + 28 99	96 + 3 99	70 + 18 88
55 + 33 88	16 + 82 98	35 + 64 99	17 + 42 59	81 + 17 98	13 + 15 28
64 + 24 88	78 + 11 89	22 + 65 87	14 + 33 47	40 + 50 90	60 + 15 75
18 + 41 59	44 + 22 66	15 + 44 59	49 + 30 79	19 + 50 69	43 + 16 59

354

Weather Report: Snowy
Subtract. Connect the dots in order from least to greatest to find the hidden picture.

Start 5 - 5 = 0

4 - 3 = 1   Start   4 - 3 = 1

6 - 4 = 2   5 - 3 = 2

5 - 2 = 3   7 - 4 = 3

7 - 3 = 4   8 - 4 = 4

8 - 3 = 5   6 - 1 = 5

7 - 1 = 6   8 - 2 = 6

355

Weather Chart
Use information from the graph to find the answers.

This Month's Weather

rainy	IIII IIII II
cloudy	IIII IIII
sunny	IIII IIII
windy	III
snowy	IIII

How many more days were rainy than windy? 7 - 3 = 4	How many more days were cloudy than snowy? 7 - 4 = 3
How many more days were sunny than snowy? 8 - 3 = 5	How many more days were windy than snowy? 4 - 3 = 1
How many more days were sunny than cloudy? 8 - 7 = 1	How many more days were sunny than rainy? 8 - 7 = 1

356

Be a Super Solver

1. Mary saw 4 chickens by the barn. Then she saw 3 more hiding by the gate. How many chickens did Mary see? Show your work.

____7____ chickens

2. John had 8 cookies. He gave 5 to his sister. How many cookies did John have left? Show your work.

____3____ cookies

3. Jim and Pam have 8 balls in all. Jim has 2 more than Pam.
How many balls does Jim have? __5__
How many balls does Pam have? __3__
Show your work.

357

Half For You, Half For Me

When you divide something in half, you divide it into two equal parts. For example, if you have two candy bars and you gave one to your friend, you would have given him or her one-half of what you have.

Color one-half of the items in each group below.

358

Use Good Cents
Count the money. Write each amount.

A. __25__¢

B. __21__¢

C. __27__¢

D. __19__¢

E. __36__¢

F. __41__¢

359

Circle Up
Circle the coins to show each amount.

35¢   20¢

14¢   43¢

25¢   54¢

30¢   47¢

360

Time Flies
Draw hands on the clocks.

12:00   4:30

8:00   5:30   7:00

6:30   3:00   9:30

361

Bar Graph Fun
Fill in the bar graph for the correct number of toys in each category.

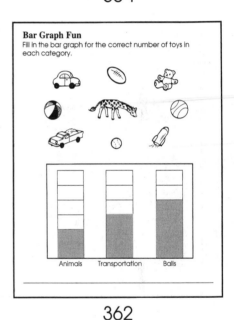

Animals   Transportation   Balls

362

An Inch Is an Inch
Cut the ruler from the bottom of the page. Measure each object to the nearest inch. Write the number of inches on each line.

A. __2 inches__   B. __4 inches__

C. __4 inches__   D. __3 inches__

1 2 3 4 5 6 7

363

Plants (continued)
Answer the questions.

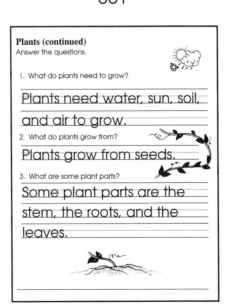

1. What do plants need to grow?

Plants need water, sun, soil, and air to grow.

2. What do plants grow from?

Plants grow from seeds.

3. What are some plant parts?

Some plant parts are the stem, the roots, and the leaves.

366

What's in the Garden?
Color these things found in a garden.
Use the number key to help you.

7 = green   8 = red   9 = orange

orange
red
red
green
orange
green
orange
green
green

369

370

Letter Mix-Up

The farm animals' names are all mixed up.
Help Robin spell them correctly on the line
beside each "mixed-up" word.

1. wco : **cow**

2. sehor : **horse**   7. nhe : **hen**

3. eepsh : **sheep**   8. ckdu : **duck**

4. oatg : **goat**   9. keyrut : **turkey**

5. tac : **cat**   10. gdo : **dog**

6. terroos : **rooster**   11. gpl : **pig**

371

You Decide
Circle yes or no.

1. Does a dog have two ears? (yes) no

2. Can a frog push a truck? yes (no)

3. Will a fox eat a bird? (yes) no

4. Do pigs have wings? yes (no)

5. Will a seal eat a fish? (yes) no

6. Can a turtle fly? yes (no)

7. Can a seal swim? (yes) no

8. Can a cat read? yes (no)

9. Do giraffes have long necks? (yes) no

372

What Belongs at the Zoo?
Color the animals.
Draw a **red** circle around the animals that live at home.
Draw a **blue** square around the animals that live at the zoo.

373

Step into the Wild
Write the name of each zoo animal.
Use the word bank to help.

1. **l i o n**

2. **h i p p o**

3. **t i g e r**

4. **m o n k e y**

5. **z e b r a**

6. **g i r a f f e**

Word Bank
monkey   hippo   lion   zebra   tiger   giraffe

376

A Snake Story

The zookeeper said, "Well, these
snakes are safely locked behind the
glass. Snakes don't want to hurt
anybody. They're just trying to
survive. But sometimes people
scare them, so they try to defend
themselves. That's when people
can get hurt."

The zookeeper left, and Tim, Kate, and
their dad stared into the cage. The snakes stared back.

"I guess you're not scared anymore, Tim," said Kate.

"Well, once you learn about something, it's not as scary.
Besides, they are behind glass!" replied Tim. They all
laughed together.

Answer "T" for true or "F" for false.

1. Snakes eat popcorn. **F**

2. Snakes are slimy. **F**

3. Snakes might hurt you when trying to defend themselves.
   T

4. Tim ran away from the snakes. **F**

5. After Tim learned about the snakes, he wasn't afraid
   anymore. **T**

377

A Ladybug Story

Read the story. Then answer the questions
that follow.

Ladybugs are insects. Ladybugs hatch from
eggs. As they grow, they change in color from pale
orange to red with black spots. Ladybugs eat aphids.
Aphids are little green bugs that live on roses
and other plants. Ladybugs can fly because
they have wings. The red part of a ladybug's
body is called the "wing case." They do not fly
very fast. Ladybugs sleep through the winter under piles of
leaves. In the spring, ladybugs wake up. Time to get busy,
ladybugs!

1. What are ladybugs? **Lady bugs are insects.**

2. What do ladybugs eat? **They eat aphids.**

3. What are aphids? **Aphids are little green bugs.**

4. What is the red part of a ladybug's body called?

   It is called a wing case.

5. What do ladybugs do during the winter? **They**

   sleep under piles of leaves.

378

For the Birds

Winter, spring, summer, fall,
all the robins do is call,
for spring, summer, fall, winter,
huddled in their nests a-twitter.
Summer, fall, winter, spring,
can't help themselves, they must sing,
through fall, winter, spring, summer,
teaching me to be a hummer.
Hum, hum, hum, hum, hum, hum, hum!
Hum, hum, hum, hum, hum, hum, hum!
Color each picture, then write the season underneath.

spring   **winter**

_mer   **fall**

381

Found in Space
Read each riddle. Write the answer.

float
stars
Mars
sun
Earth
craters
shuttle
Saturn

1. This huge star lights the day. **s u n**

2. These shine at night. **s t a r s**

3. These are on the moon. **c r a t e r s**

4. This is our home planet. **E a r t h**

5. This flies into space. **s h u t t l e**

6. This planet is red. **M a r s**

7. This planet has rings. **S a t u r n**

8. Astronauts do this in space. **f l o a t**

382

The Space Shuttle
Read the story.

The space shuttle takes astronauts
into space. Rockets launch the
shuttle. The shuttle orbits the earth.
The astronauts do work in space.
They may set up satellites or do
experiments. When it is time to
return, the shuttle lands on a
runway. The astronauts are back
on earth.

Answer the questions.

1. What takes astronauts into space? **The space shuttle**
   takes astronauts into space.

2. What launches the shuttle into space? **Rockets**
   launch the shuttle into space.

3. What kind of work do astronauts do in space? **They**
   may set up satellites or do experiments.

4. Where does the shuttle land when it returns to earth?
   The shuttle lands on a runway.

Fossil Find

Draw a line to match the fossil imprint with the object that made it.

383

Dinosaur Giants

The biggest dinosaurs were plant-eaters. They had heavy legs and big bodies. Their heads were small but their necks were long.

These huge dinosaurs had to eat a lot of food. They may have walked very far to find all the food they needed.

They used their long necks to eat food at the tops of trees. They may have even stood on their hind legs to get food.

Can you find these words in the puzzle? Circle each one.

☐ huge ☐ food
☐ body ☐ walk
☐ head ☐ eat
☐ neck ☐ legs

b	r	l	e	g	s	r
o	m	h	r	w	p	d
d	z	u	l	a	m	h
y	o	g	d	l	e	e
a	n	e	c	k	v	a
e	a	t	f	o	o	d

384

Dinosaur Riddles

Read each riddle.
Draw a line to the matching picture.

I had a big head.
I had long, sharp teeth.
Who am I?

I had a big head.
I had three sharp horns.
Who am I?

I had a small head.
I had a long, long neck.
Who am I?

I had a mouth like a duck.
I had a long crest.
Who am I?

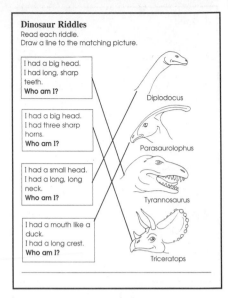

Diplodocus

Parasaurolophus

Tyrannosaurus

Triceratops

385

Dining Manners

Help Polite Pig teach his friends some table manners. Write the missing word to begin each rule. Draw a line from the rule to the friend who needs to learn it.

Word Bank
Chew   Cut
Put   Use

Chew with your mouth closed.

Use a spoon or fork to eat most foods.

Cut your food into bite-size pieces.

Put your napkin on your lap to begin.

388

What Is Happening?

Circle the names of things in the picture.

(fossils)   (tools)   dog
snowman   (workers)   (camera)
(dirt)   (hat)   money

Circle and write the best title for the picture.

Hiking in the Desert   (Finding Fossils)   At the Museum

Finding Fossils

389

Community Workers

Read each riddle.
Draw a line to the matching picture.

I come to your house.
I bring something.
It has a stamp.
Who am I?

I work in a store.
I help you find things.
I take your money.
Who am I?

I work at the pool.
I am a good swimmer.
I can save lives.
Who am I?

I start early each day,
I mix up some dough.
Then I bake it.
Who am I?

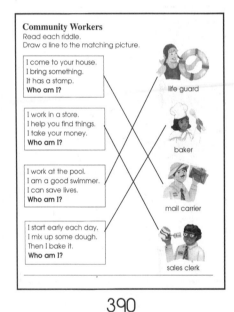

life guard

baker

mail carrier

sales clerk

390

Where Do They Work?

Cut out the community workers.
Paste them on the map at the places where they work.

391

Getting There

The children are walking through the town square to the bus stop. Draw a line to show the path they will take.

393

A Busy Community

People live, work, and play together in a community.
Look at each picture. Circle the sentence that matches it.

They will ride their bikes.
(They will ride the bus.)

They are going shopping.
(They are going to the park.)

(Someone needs help.)
Someone is late.

The library is open.
(The library is closed.)

The firefighters are playing.
(The firefighters are working.)

(It is a school day.)
It is a weekend day.

396

Daily Learning Drills Grad

Recycle It!

...e pictures show a busy day at a recycling center.
...you find **10** differences between the two pictures?

What does your family or your community recycle?

_____

_____

397

Community Center

Have you ever been to a community center? At a community center, you can do many fun things.

You can take an art class or learn how to swim. There might be a gym where people can exercise.

At my community center there is a special wall. Kids can learn to rock climb on the wall!

Can you find these words in the puzzle?
Circle each one.

☐ center ☐ class

☐ learn ☐ swim

☐ gym ☐ climb

☐ wall ☐ fun

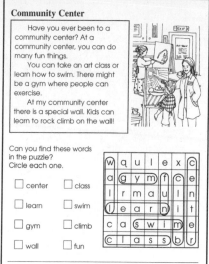

398

In the Mountains

Read the story.

Have you ever been to a mountain community? Most mountain communities are far from busy cities. Some people live in the mountains all year. Other people visit the mountains on vacation. In the winter, they ski or play in the snow. In the summer they might rest, hike, and ride bikes.

Finish the sentences.

1. Most mountain communities are __far__ from busy cities.

2. Some people live in the mountains all __year__.

3. In the __winter__, people like to ski.

4. In the summer, they might ride __bikes__.

399

Good Citizens

Write the word that completes each sentence.

Vote Today

1. Good citizens obey the __laws__

   laws
   cats

2. They __help__ their communities.

   ride
   help

3. Good citizens care for __earth__

   happy
   earth

4. They try to be good __neighbors__

   neighbors
   shoes

5. They vote for their __leaders__

   floor
   leaders

6. You can be a good __citizen__

   car
   citizen

400

Some Super Signs

Look at each sign. Read the questions. Circle the correct answers.

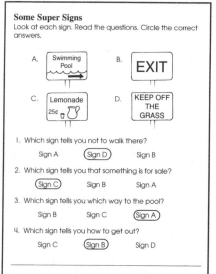

A. Swimming Pool
B. EXIT
C. Lemonade 25¢
D. KEEP OFF THE GRASS

1. Which sign tells you not to walk there?

   Sign A   (Sign D)   Sign B

2. Which sign tells you that something is for sale?

   (Sign C)   Sign B   Sign A

3. Which sign tells you which way to the pool?

   Sign B   Sign C   (Sign A)

4. Which sign tells you how to get out?

   Sign C   (Sign B)   Sign D

401

African Life

Color and cut out these pictures of African life. Divide the pictures into two piles, one for traditional items and the other for modern items.

403

Name _____

Some Super Signs

Look at each sign. Read the questions. Circle the correct answers.

A.

B.

C.

D.

1. Which sign tells you not to walk there?

    Sign A   Sign D   Sign B

2. Which sign tells you that something is for sale?

    Sign C   Sign B   Sign A

3. Which sign tells you which way to the pool?

    Sign B   Sign C   Sign A

4. Which sign tells you how to get out?

    Sign C   Sign B   Sign D

SOCIAL STUDIES REVIEW

Name _____

Map Activity

Follow the directions to color the map of Kenya.

1. Draw a wooden sailboat in the Indian Ocean.
2. Color the Great Rift Valley brown.
3. Draw a blue star where Nairobi is marked.
4. Color the dome-shaped hut red.
5. Color Lake Turkana and Lake Victoria blue.

Name _____

African Life

Color and cut out these pictures of African life. Divide the pictures into two piles, one for traditional items and the other for modern items.

SOCIAL STUDIES REVIEW

Daily Learning Drills Grade 1

Review Answer Key

ABC Planets
Write the names of the planets in ABC order.

1. Earth
2. Jupiter
3. Mars
4. Mercury
5. Neptune
6. Pluto
7. Saturn
8. Uranus
9. Venus

321

3-2-1 Blastoff!
Find and circle 9 hidden pictures that begin with **b**.

book   bell   bat
bus   bib   bow
ball   bone   bun

322

An Icy Path
Help the penguins get to the iceberg. Say the name of each picture on the path. Circle the beginning sound.

323

Up, Up, and Away!
Look at the pictures behind each plane. Color the pictures that begin with the sound of the letter on the plane.

324

Hooray for Consonants!
Say the name of each picture. Write the letter that makes the beginning sound.

m   b   w
f   h   s   d
r   g   p   l
w   n   t

325

Animals, Animals
Say the name of each animal. Circle the letter that makes the ending sound. Then color the pictures.

326

Plucky's Pictures
Plucky Duck drew pictures of things that have a short **u** sound. Look at the pictures below. Which ones did Plucky draw? Color them.

327

Rainy Day Puddles
Look at the pictures on the umbrellas. Write their names on the puddles. Use the words on the rain cloud.

cup sun jug rug
bus nut bug duck

rug   bug
cup   nut   sun
jug   duck   bus

328

What's Hiding?
Find out what is hiding below. If a space has a picture of a short **o** word, color it red. Color the other spaces yellow.

What was hiding? _____ 0

329

Hunt for Short O
Dottie Fox looked in her home for things that have short **o** in their names. Read the list she made. Write each word under the matching picture.

pot   top
mop   doll
box   sock
lock   clock

top   pot
clock lock   mop
box   doll   sock

Name the Pictures
Label the pictures below.
Use the words in the box.

cake gate tape
rake vase cane
cape cave game

rake   cave   tape
gate   vase   game
cake   cape   cane

What Will They Do?
Look at the picture clues. Write the correct word for each sentence.

1. Dale will bake a __cake__
   cake cane

2. Jane will swim in the __lake__
   late lake

3. Nate will play a __game__
   game gate

4. Dave will help Dad __rake__
   rate rake

5. Kate will wash the __plate__
   plate place

6. Jake will __skate__ at the rink.
   skate snake

330

331

332

Let's Read Long "e" Words!
Look at each picture.
Write the long **e** word.

Long e Words
bead   read
dream seal
leaf   wheat
peach

l e a f
read   d r e a m
s e a l   p e a c h
b e a d   w h e a t

Hidden Picture Fun
Can you find **9** hidden pictures of **long i** words? Circle them.

bike   kite   nine
five   lime   pipe
hive   dime   slide

Let's Sail
Write the answer to each riddle.
Use the long **a** words in the box.

mail nail pail
sail tail wail

1. This is part of a boat.   2. A dog wags this.
   __sail__   __tail__

3. It carries water.   4. You hit this with a hammer.
   __pail__   __nail__

5. You can read this.   6. This means "to cry."
   __mail__   __wail__

333

334

335

A Cute Mule
Circle the long **u** word that matches each picture.

cute / rule   tube / dune
mule / prune   dude / glue
Sue / cube   fume / June
blue / tune   flute / rude

Rhyme Time Fun
Look at the pictures.
Write a sentence that tells about each picture.
Hint: Each sentence will have two rhyming long **o** words.

toad
road
boat
moat
coat
goat

A __boat__ is in the __moat__.

The __goat__ is wearing a __coat__.

A __toad__ is on the __road__.

Words and Meanings
Read the two words on each dinosaur.
If they have the same meaning, color the dinosaur **green**.
If they do not have the same meaning, color the dinosaur **red**.

green   green
red
green
green
green
red   green

336

337

338

Compound It
Draw lines between pairs of words to make compound words. Then write the words.

pine   corn   **popcorn**

bird   apple   **pineapple**

hot   ball   **football**

pop   dog   **hotdog**

foot   house   **birdhouse**

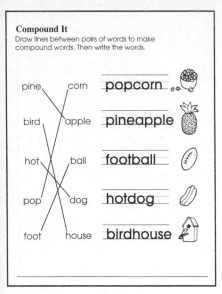

339

Space Questions
Questions often begin with these words.

Who
What
When
Where
Why

Complete each sentence with the correct word from the box.

1. **Who** can become an astronaut?

2. **Why** do people want to be astronauts?

3. **Where** is the space shuttle kept?

4. **When** will there be a shuttle launch?

5. **What** do astronauts wear in space?

340

On the Moon
Circle the sentences that tell about the picture.
Write them on the lines. Read the story.

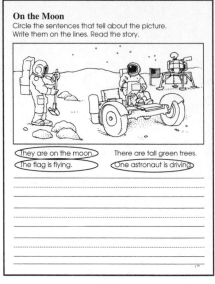

They are on the moon.   There are tall green trees.
The flag is flying.   One astronaut is driving.

341

Gentle Giraffes
Color the circles.
Then color the rest of the picture.

342

Roarin' Rhino
Color the triangles. Then color the rest of the picture.

Rhinoceros

343

Polar Bear Palace
Circle the 6 mistakes in the picture. Color.

344

Perfect Peacocks
Count the number of feathers on each peacock.
Write the number on the line.

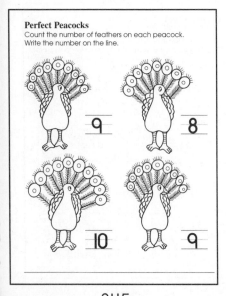

9   8

10   9

345

Hum a Sweet Tune
Connect the dots from 1 to 20. Color.

346

Fill It In
Write in the missing numbers.

1	2	3	4	5	6	7	8	9	10
11	12	13	14	15	16	17	18	19	20
21	22	23	24	25	26	27	28	29	30
31	32	33	34	35	36	37	38	39	40
41	42	43	44	45	46	47	48	49	50
51	52	53	54	55	56	57	58	59	60
61	62	63	64	65	66	67	68	69	70
71	72	73	74	75	76	77	78	79	80
81	82	83	84	85	86	87	88	89	90
91	92	93	94	95	96	97	98	99	100

347

Even More Fun!

Find the even number words hidden in the puzzle. Words go across, down, and diagonally. Use the Word Bank to help you.

Word Bank

two	twelve
four	fourteen
six	sixteen
eight	eighteen
ten	

```
a b f b d i j a q a r a
w f e w e f o u r t e e n
c o d l e h a z p d s b w
v u g u d l s i x t e e n
c r k m h v o z i w l h
l x e i g h t e e n t o y
d e n y m e y n s i x o p
```

348

Garden Friends

Circle the animal that comes next in each row.

349

What Comes Next?

Complete each pattern by drawing a picture in the blank.

350

Blast Off!

Count by 2s to complete the picture and find out where your imagination can take you! Then color the picture.

351

Rockin' Roller Coaster

Write numbers on the cars, counting by 5s.

352

Swift Swimmers

Add. Color the spaces on the fish that match each sum as you go. The fish to be completely covered is the fastest swimmer.

5	7	2	6	3
+ 3	+ 5	+ 0	+ 4	+ 2
8	12	2	10	5

6	5	6	3	3
+ 5	+ 2	+ 3	+ 3	+ 1
11	7	9	6	4

353

What's the Scoop?

Add.

12	11	54	71	96	70
+ 3	+ 12	+ 32	+ 28	+ 3	+ 18
15	23	86	99	99	88

55	16	35	17	81	13
+ 33	+ 82	+ 64	+ 42	+ 17	+ 15
88	98	99	59	98	28

64	78	22	14	40	60
+ 24	+ 11	+ 65	+ 33	+ 50	+ 15
88	89	87	47	90	75

18	44	15	49	19	43
+ 41	+ 22	+ 44	+ 30	+ 50	+ 16
59	66	59	79	69	59

354

Weather Report: Snowy

Subtract. Connect the dots in order from least to greatest to find the hidden picture.

Start 5 - 5 = 0
Start 4 - 3 = 1
4 - 3 = 1
6 - 4 = 2
5 - 3 = 2
5 - 2 = 3
7 - 4 = 3
7 - 3 = 4
8 - 4 = 4
8 - 3 = 5
6 - 1 = 5
7 - 1 = 6
8 - 2 = 6

355

Weather Chart

Use information from the graph to find the answers.

This Month's Weather

rainy	
cloudy	
sunny	
windy	
snowy	

How many more days were ☔ than 💨?	How many more days were ☁ than 💨?
7 - 3 = 4	7 - 4 = 3

How many more days were ☀ than 💨?	How many more days were ❄ than 💨?
8 - 3 = 5	4 - 3 = 1

How many more days were ☀ than ☁?	How many more days were ☀ than ☔?
8 - 7 = 1	8 - 7 = 1

356

Be a Super Solver

1. Mary saw 4 chickens by the barn. Then she saw 3 more hiding by the gate. How many chickens did Mary see? Show your work.

__7__ chickens

2. John had 8 cookies. He gave 5 to his sister. How many cookies did John have left? Show your work.

__3__ cookies

3. Jim and Pam have 8 balls in all. Jim has 2 more than Pam.
How many balls does Jim have? __5__
How many balls does Pam have? __3__
Show your work.

357

Half For You, Half For Me
When you divide something in half, you divide it into two equal parts. For example, if you have two candy bars and you gave one to your friend, you would have given him or her one-half of what you have.

Color one-half of the items in each group below.

358

Use Good Cents
Count the money. Write each amount.

A. __25__¢

B. __21__¢

C. __27__¢

D. __19__¢

E. __36__¢

F. __41__¢

359

Circle Up
Circle the coins to show each amount.

35¢   20¢

14¢   43¢

25¢   54¢

30¢   47¢

360

Time Flies
Draw hands on the clocks.

12:00   4:30

8:00   5:30   7:00

6:30   3:00   9:30

361

Bar Graph Fun
Fill in the bar graph for the correct number of toys in each category.

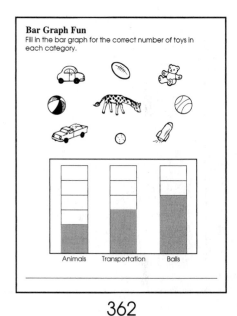

Animals   Transportation   Balls

362

An Inch Is an Inch
Cut the ruler from the bottom of the page. Measure each object to the nearest inch. Write the number of inches on each line.

A. __2 inches__   B. __4 inches__

C. __4 inches__   D. __3 inches__

363

Plants (continued)
Answer the questions.

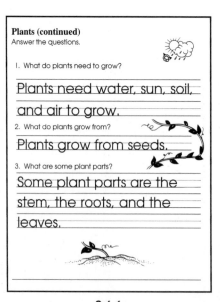

1. What do plants need to grow?

Plants need water, sun, soil, and air to grow.

2. What do plants grow from?

Plants grow from seeds.

3. What are some plant parts?

Some plant parts are the stem, the roots, and the leaves.

366

What's in the Garden?
Color these things found in a garden.
Use the number key to help you.

7 = green   8 = red   9 = orange

369

Letter Mix-Up

Help! The farm animals' names are all mixed up. Help Robin spell them correctly on the line beside each "mixed-up" word.

1. wco : __cow__

2. sehor : __horse__   7. nhe : __hen__

3. eepsh : __sheep__   8. ckdu : __duck__

4. oatg : __goat__   9. keyrut : __turkey__

5. tac : __cat__   10. gdo : __dog__

6. terroos : __rooster__   11. gpi : __pig__

370

You Decide

Circle yes or no.

1. Does a dog have two ears? (yes) no
2. Can a frog push a truck? yes (no)
3. Will a fox eat a bird? (yes) no
4. Do pigs have wings? yes (no)
5. Will a seal eat a fish? (yes) no
6. Can a turtle fly? yes (no)
7. Can a seal swim? (yes) no
8. Can a cat read? yes (no)
9. Do giraffes have long necks? (yes) no

371

What Belongs at the Zoo?

Color the animals.
Draw a **red** circle around the animals that live at home.
Draw a **blue** square around the animals that live at the zoo.

372

Step into the Wild

Write the name of each zoo animal.
Use the word bank to help.

1. __l i o n__
2. __h i p p o__
3. __t i g e r__
4. __m o n k e y__
5. __z e b r a__
6. __g i r a f f e__

Word Bank
monkey   hippo   lion   zebra   tiger   giraffe

373

A Snake Story

The zookeeper said, "Well, these snakes are safely locked behind the glass. Snakes don't want to hurt anybody. They're just trying to survive. But sometimes people scare them, so they try to defend themselves. That's when people can get hurt."

The zookeeper left, and Tim, Kate, and their dad stared into the cage. The snakes stared back.

"I guess you're not scared anymore, Tim," said Kate.

"Well, once you learn about something, it's not as scary. Besides, they are behind glass!" replied Tim. They all laughed together.

Answer "T" for true or "F" for false.

1. Snakes eat popcorn. __F__
2. Snakes are slimy. __F__
3. Snakes might hurt you when trying to defend themselves. __T__
4. Tim ran away from the snakes. __F__
5. After Tim learned about the snakes, he wasn't afraid anymore. __T__

376

A Ladybug Story

Read the story. Then answer the questions that follow.

Ladybugs are insects. Ladybugs hatch from eggs. As they grow, they change in color from pale orange to red with black spots. Ladybugs eat aphids. Aphids are little green bugs that live on roses and other plants. Ladybugs can fly because they have wings. The red part of a ladybug's body is called the "wing case." They do not fly very fast. Ladybugs sleep through the winter under piles of leaves. In the spring, ladybugs wake up. Time to get busy, ladybugs!

1. What are ladybugs? __Lady bugs are insects.__
2. What do ladybugs eat? __They eat aphids.__
3. What are aphids? __Aphids are little green bugs.__
4. What is the red part of a ladybug's body called?
__It is called a wing case.__
5. What do ladybugs do during the winter? __They__
__sleep under piles of leaves.__

377

For the Birds

Winter, spring, summer, fall,
all the robins do is call,
for spring, summer, fall, winter,
huddled in their nests a-twitter.
Summer, fall, winter, spring,
can't help themselves, they must sing,
through fall, winter, spring, summer,
teaching me to be a hummer.
Hum, hum, hum, hum, hum, hum, hum!
Hum, hum, hum, hum, hum, hum, hum!

Color each picture, then write the season underneath.

spring   winter

summer   fall

378

Found in Space

Read each riddle. Write the answer.

float
stars
Mars
sun
Earth
craters
shuttle
Saturn

1. This huge star lights the day. __s u n__
2. These shine at night. __s t a r s__
3. These are on the moon. __c r a t e r s__
4. This is our home planet. __E a r t h__
5. This flies into space. __s h u t t l e__
6. This planet is red. __M a r s__
7. This planet has rings. __S a t u r n__
8. Astronauts do this in space. __f l o a t__

381

The Space Shuttle

Read the story.

The space shuttle takes astronauts into space. Rockets launch the shuttle. The shuttle orbits the earth. The astronauts do work in space. They may set up satellites or do experiments. When it is time to return, the shuttle lands on a runway. The astronauts are back on earth.

Answer the questions.

1. What takes astronauts into space? __The space shuttle__ __takes astronauts into space.__
2. What launches the shuttle into space? __Rockets__ __launch the shuttle into space.__
3. What kind of work do astronauts do in space? __They__ __may set up satellites or do experiments.__
4. Where does the shuttle land when it returns to earth? __The shuttle lands on a runway.__

382

Fossil Find
Draw a line to match the fossil imprint with the object that made it.

383

Dinosaur Giants

The biggest dinosaurs were plant-eaters. They had heavy legs and big bodies. Their heads were small but their necks were long.

These huge dinosaurs had to eat a lot of food. They may have walked very far to find all the food they needed.

They used their long necks to eat food at the tops of trees. They may have even stood on their hind legs to get food.

Can you find these words in the puzzle? Circle each one.

☐ huge   ☐ food
☐ body   ☐ walk
☐ head   ☐ eat
☐ neck   ☐ legs

b	r	l	e	g	s	r
o	m	h	r	w	p	d
d	z	u	l	a	m	h
y	o	g	d	l	e	e
a	n	e	c	k	v	a
e	a	t	f	o	o	d

384

Dinosaur Riddles
Read each riddle.
Draw a line to the matching picture.

I had a big head.
I had long, sharp teeth.
Who am I?

I had a big head.
I had three sharp horns.
Who am I?

I had a small head.
I had a long, long neck.
Who am I?

I had a mouth like a duck.
I had a long crest.
Who am I?

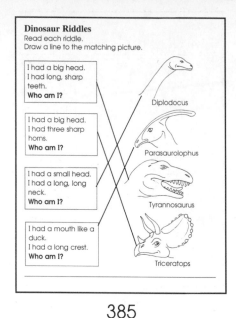

Diplodocus

Parasaurolophus

Tyrannosaurus

Triceratops

385

Dining Manners
Help Polite Pig teach his friends some table manners. Write the missing word to begin each rule. Draw a line from the rule to the friend who needs to learn it.

Word Bank
Chew   Cut
Put   Use

Chew with your mouth closed.

Use a spoon or fork to eat most foods.

Cut your food into bite-size pieces.

Put your napkin on your lap to begin.

388

What Is Happening?

Circle the names of things in the picture.

(fossils)   (tools)   dog
snowman   (workers)   (camera)
(dirt)   (hat)   money

Circle and write the best title for the picture.

Hiking in the Desert   (Finding Fossils)   At the Museum

Finding Fossils

389

Community Workers
Read each riddle.
Draw a line to the matching picture.

I come to your house.
I bring something.
It has a stamp.
Who am I?

I work in a store.
I help you find things.
I take your money.
Who am I?

I work at the pool.
I am a good swimmer.
I can save lives.
Who am I?

I start early each day.
I mix up some dough.
Then I bake it.
Who am I?

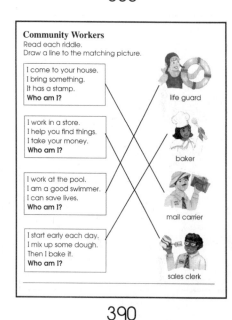

life guard

baker

mail carrier

sales clerk

390

Where Do They Work?
Cut out the community workers.
Paste them on the map at the places where they work.

391

Getting There
The children are walking through the town square to the bus stop. Draw a line to show the path they will take.

393

A Busy Community
People live, work, and play together in a community.
Look at each picture. Circle the sentence that matches it.

They will ride their bikes.
(They will ride the bus.)

They are going shopping.
(They are going to the park.)

(Someone needs help.)
Someone is late.

The library is open.
(The library is closed.)

The firefighters are playing.
(The firefighters are working.)

(It is a school day.)
It is a weekend day.

396

Recycle It!

These pictures show a busy day at a recycling center. Can you find **10** differences between the two pictures?

What does your family or your community recycle?

_____
_____
_____

Community Center

Have you ever been to a community center? At a community center, you can do many fun things.

You can take an art class or learn how to swim. There might be a gym where people can exercise.

At my community center there is a special wall. Kids can learn to rock climb on the wall!

Can you find these words in the puzzle? Circle each one.

☐ center   ☐ class

☐ learn   ☐ swim

☐ gym   ☐ climb

☐ wall   ☐ fun

w	q	u	l	e	x	c
a	g	y	m	f	c	e
l	r	m	a	u	l	n
l	e	a	r	n	i	t
c	a	s	w	i	m	e
c	l	a	s	s	b	r

In the Mountains

Read the story.

Have you ever been to a mountain community? Most mountain communities are far from busy cities. Some people live in the mountains all year. Other people visit the mountains on vacation. In the winter, they ski or play in the snow. In the summer they might rest, hike, and ride bikes.

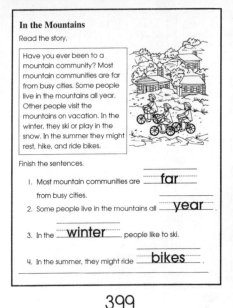

Finish the sentences.

1. Most mountain communities are ___far___ from busy cities.

2. Some people live in the mountains all ___year___.

3. In the ___winter___, people like to ski.

4. In the summer, they might ride ___bikes___.

Good Citizens

Write the word that completes each sentence.

Vote Today

1. Good citizens obey the ___laws___ .

| laws |
| cats |

2. They ___help___ their communities.

| ride |
| help |

3. Good citizens care for ___earth___ .

| happy |
| earth |

4. They try to be good ___neighbors___ .

| neighbors |
| shoes |

5. They vote for their ___leaders___ .

| floor |
| leaders |

6. You can be a good ___citizen___ .

| car |
| citizen |

Some Super Signs

Look at each sign. Read the questions. Circle the correct answers.

A. Swimming Pool →

B. EXIT

C. Lemonade 25¢

D. KEEP OFF THE GRASS

1. Which sign tells you not to walk there?

Sign A   (Sign D)   Sign B

2. Which sign tells you that something is for sale?

(Sign C)   Sign B   Sign A

3. Which sign tells you which way to the pool?

Sign B   Sign C   (Sign A)

4. Which sign tells you how to get out?

Sign C   (Sign B)   Sign D

African Life

Color and cut out these pictures of African life. Divide the pictures into two piles, one for traditional items and the other for modern items.